RUMINATIONS

A MOSAIC OF ESSAYS

DAVELLA PASHUPATI

I dedicate this book to my friend, Dr Sabina Fatima Hussain, who has known me all my life.

She motivated me to compile my thought processes, complete this book and publish this volume.

She assisted through review and proofreading and offered constructive suggestions.

I am thankful to Dr Sabina Fatima Hussain.

Contents

Contents

Contents

Contents

Over the years, I have been writing on socio-economic topics and stories from my growing-up days. Some of these were compiled in my maiden book, "*The House Under a Neem Tree*." The book was well received, and I am grateful to those who could find time to read it and offer constructive suggestions.

Meanwhile, I continue to write. Writing is not only a creative expression; it also helps clarify one's thought processes. One feels more complete when writing, revising, revisiting, and sometimes altering one's stand.

So, here is my second book, which is a collection of my ruminations over a period of time. It contains various essays on society, people, polity, governance, education, judiciary, environment, religion, faith and personal reflections.

While compiling my write-ups, I realised how anthropocentric we humans are. In our scriptures, we allude to humans as the apex of God's creation. We have started believing that the Earth belongs to us alone and all other creatures are at our mercy. We have, therefore, exterminated creatures which do not serve our purposes and domesticated what we needed. We even went beyond and started playing with Mother Earth for our purposes. All these are simply because we have higher cranium capacity, can organise better, and have mastered the technology to reap our narrow benefits. Our anthropocentricity leads to me first, my gender, my family, my tribe/caste, my political propensity, my country and my religion. In other words, we are the best and have all the rights to our greed and avarice. We have started believing in our superiority and our immortality and have started stealing from our coming generation, too.

For the first time, emerging technologies, including artificial intelligence and increased automation, have made us realise that we humans may become redundant, which should be a sobering thought. No other creature, or even Earth, needs us as much as we need them. Happily, we can see silver linings in the otherwise dark, cloudy night. We have started to behave more responsibly. Some of my write-ups allude to this.

I am inclined to quote this childhood poem by Mrs G. S. Virle, who ran a play school in our locality. She was a war widow, and this school kept her engaged. Making money was not her priority. The times were different...

All of us from our family went to her school and were taught this poem. Now, this is some kind of family poem. We all learnt our alphabet at her play school, and only through the alphabet can one express oneself. Every epic writing starts with a dot, as they say.

माना तुम ताक़त वाले हो
रखते हो बल हाथी का।
फिर भी करे भरोसा कैसे
ताक़त जैसे साथी का।

हाथी का घमंड भी
छोड़ा सा अंकुश।
कर देता है चूर!
बड़े बड़े ताक़त वाले भी
क्षण में हो जाते है चूर।

माना तुम रूपवान हो
लाखों में एक मनोहर हो!
फिर भी करे भरोसा कैसे
जो रूप स्वयं ही नश्वर हो!

काम ना देता किस तरह बल
और एक दिन आता है
जब मनुष्य भी रोगी होकर शक्तिहीन हो जाता है.

[English translation
I admit you're strong, with power untold,
You possess the strength of an elephant, bold.
But how can one trust, as one trusts a friend,
The might you wield, which may one-day end?
The pride of an elephant, so grand,
A goad can make it stumble and land.

Even the mighty, with power so pure,
Can falter in a moment, unsure and insecure.
I admit you're handsome, a beauty so rare,
In a million, none like you, beyond compare!
But how can one trust, in beauty's grace,
When even looks vanish, time leaves no trace?
Power may fade, and beauty may wane,
But friendship, true, will always remain.
When strength is fleeting and beauty may die,
A companion's love will never pass by]
- with remembrance and thanks to Late Mrs Virle.

]

I hope you will like this mosaic of essays.
Do give your feedback to pashupati@gmail.com.
Bangalore
30th of March 2025

Acknowledgements

I sincerely thank Mr Sundaresan Jagannivasan, an abstract artist, for allowing me to use his oil canvas painting for my book cover. Mr Jagannivasan is a wonderful, affectionate human being, and I am fortunate to live in the same building.

The oil on canvas painting, measuring 36 inches * 48 inches, is titled "*Collective Vibrations*" by the artist. It signifies that the entire cosmos is vibrating synchronously. It aligns well with my belief that the entire universe is but one Prana (Collective Universal Consciousness), which experiences different facets of existence and manifests itself through different lives and objects and, at the end of it, merges back into the same collective consciousness. Our body is just a host and a temporary residence for a part of Pranic existence.

I thank my college mate and friend Jaskaranan Singh Bhogal for making and sharing his sketches for this book. Jaskaran is a successful IT entrepreneur who dabbles in sketching.

Finally, I thank my mother for encouraging me to complete this work more than once. She is dependent, and on several occasions, she waited patiently for me to complete my write-up before I could help her.

Finally, I thank all my family members, friends, and well-wishers who read my book, '*The House Under a Neem Tree*' and my blogs and encouraged me to compile my write-ups into a book.

SOCIETY & PEOPLE

1

Year of Hope

I'm happy to see the passing of a year,
    More of a tragic play like King Lear,
    Most of the time spent in one's lair,
    Endlessly worrying about near and dear,
    Watching less laughter more a tear,
    Mindfully meditating on now and here,
    Mercifully, on the horizon,
    light appears crystal clear.

Let us now stop looking at the side flip,
    Aberration it was, just a mere blip,
    Miles to go, have promises to keep,
    Before we even consider sleep,
    Let the future be rosy and pass off in a slip,
    Revelry, dancing in hop and hip,
    Savour the Elixir of Life in little sips,
    With devotion & prayers on our lips.

We have a fresh canvas with a new scope,
    With palms joined in submission and hope,
    Lord, show us light so we can cope,
    Do not leave us in darkness to grope,
    And don't make us while away time in mope.

So, at the midnight stroke.
   Let a new dawn begin,
   Let a new era usher,

Welcome, to the brand new year.
   P.S. - I wrote this poem, the year Covid 19 ended. It was such a great relief to be alive and enter a new year, for most of us.

2

Gross Consumerism

He who buys what he does not need steals from himself.
- Swedish Proverb

My mother's hand-sewing machine is a late fifties vintage. It is made of solid iron and metal and is heavy to lift. But it works well even today and looks new. When I visited a shop recently, I was disappointed to see the quality of the latest generation of machines. Though technologically superior, these appeared so flimsy that I doubted they could last even a decade. A decade?

Stainless steel vessels from my mother's marriage time look new. The best ones you buy today start cracking within a few years.

The Burma teak furniture at home, modest in design and comfort, lasted a lifetime and more. Until during a moment of brain fade, we disposed of these for modern junk—Ditto for the brass kitchen storage jars, water heaters, etc.

My ancestral home, made of 18-inch brick and mud walls, partly covered with country tiles, having an open courtyard, was designed to be well-ventilated and kept cool in the scorching north Indian summer. We could sow seeds in the foreyard, water with used kitchen water, and reap rich organic vegetables.

The bomma kolu dolls in those days were pieces of artwork and looked lifelike. The Shiva Parvathi marriage set, the South Indian marriage set, the Dasavatar set...up north, we lived in an imagined south of India, partly based on these dolls.

Imagine my disappointment when I visited Mylapore, Madras, searching for a similar set. What I found paled in comparison in terms of finesse and artwork.

What are we witnessing, and why? What has changed over the last couple of generations? Products were designed to last, so the pressure on natural resources did not reoccur. We were not cutting trees all the time.

A lot of skill and commitment went into making things then. They were designed to be appropriate for the local requirements and ambience. No one looked down upon our old furniture because everyone had a lifestyle like ours. We were in greater unison with nature, living within our means, subconsciously caring for nature, and building durable things for us and the coming generations.

Then came Pax Americana. With mad consumerism and quick churning, new models made old ones less desirable or embarrassing as things went out of fashion.

Then came Pax Sino. Cheaper but of notorious quality. Replacing was painless, as we developed no emotion for these products. And one could afford to throw away and buy new models.

The irony is that, amid this short-lived consumerism, we continue to debate global warming, exploitation of natural resources and utter shibboleths about preserving Mother Earth for coming generations.

3

Consumer Economics

All that clutter used to be money. All the money used to be time.
- Unknown

I am borrowing an old computer acronym - WYSIWYG - what you see is what you get.

Well, my experience of buying online has so far been non-WYSIWYG. The other day, I ordered a laundry bag online. The much-awaited parcel landed in a rather impressive, large pack with bubble packing (I do not know why). It looked exactly as in the picture but was rather flimsy. I felt that it would not last long.

"But why do you want it to last long? If it wears out, buy a new one. It's just Rs 900." the young one told me.

Now, that is the brilliance of consumer economics and the virtues of a vibrant and confident society. We have converted semi-assets like clothes into consumer goods. Earlier, we would maintain and pamper clothes. Now, they are just a fashion statement. You stop wearing them, not because they have faded (in fact, you start wearing them because they are faded!), but because they are 'out of fashion'.

Flashback. We would get two or three sets of clothes a year but still try to use the old ones as long as possible. It just added to our stocks. We would go to a cobbler, get the old slippers repaired and preserve the new ones for formal occasions.

Clothes would never die. If they got old, they would first be repaired for you, fit into your younger sibling, metamorphose into a cloth bag, and finally become a floor-cleaning duster.

Thrift and frugality were in the air—we had a better word for it—wisdom. Economising was considered part of Mom's responsibility. The month-end budget stretch and cutting down on a few things, such as vegetables, were expected and readily accepted by the family.

So, coal dust would embrace wet mud, get converted into small balls called 'gul', sun-dried and end up in the coal sigdi (burner) for cooking. It would not end up there, too. The resultant ash could be used to wash vessels, and the wet sludge was an excellent garden manure.

In their afterlife, plastic buckets would become flower pots, which would then be picked up by kabadiwala in exchange for some plastic goody. Ragpickers would rummage through garden waste to pick up metal parts and other monetisable goods.

Recycling, optimisation, savings, and creative use were good words. Maybe that is why we were poor as families and as a society. Perhaps this is why we missed the growth bus.

We are now looking forward to conquering the world, powered by the nitrous oxide provided by mad consumerism. This is why clothes are stone-washed, slashed, and burned before they are worn.

That is why my flimsy laundry bag is a piece of good news.

Economists would call it the velocity of money. In the new paradigm, the less time money stays with you, the greater the multiplier effect. It gives more bang for a buck, so to speak.

It is 'cool' to borrow the appropriate term from the next generation.

Is Charvaka* alive?

* Charvaka was an ancient Indian saint who advocated epicurenism. He is credited with this saying

Yavat Jivite Sukham Jivite

Rinam Kritva ghritam pibet

Bhasmibhutasya dehasya

punragmanm kutah

[As long as you live, live happily. Take a loan, if needed and drink ghee (enjoy life). Once the body is reduced to ashes, where is the return (afterlife)?]

4
Character of a Nation

National Character is the sum of the moral fiber of its individuals. It can not be built by law
- Herbert Hoover

A friend made a very pertinent point.

While we all share jokes about demonetisation, some blame Modi and the government for its supposed failure, some even chuckle, and many are secretly happy to have outsmarted the system and converted their loot.

What does it tell about us as a nation? Anyone who could - banker, cooperative, petrol bunk, rail clerk, utility counter clerk, accountant, temple priest ...anyone who could...used this to make some money.

So, instead of working towards removing black money, millions of Indians saw in it an opportunity to create some for themselves.

Ironically, these very people will blame the government for black money and its inability to trace and punish the guilty.

If nothing else, this drive has shown us all a mirror. As a nation, how corrupt we are. If you are honest, it is more likely that you did not get a chance to get corrupt. If you got it, you made it.

I know it hurts. It hurts a lot.

It reminds me of a childhood story about a corrupt, dishonest guy throwing a party. After dinner, the guests started stealing things from the host's place. The next day, they returned the stolen stuff with an apology, except for the servant, who had become incorrigible and dishonest because he had been eating at the corrupt place forever.

Sixty years of corruption have made us all Indians corrupt. We have lost our soul and our will to remain honest. Only the body remains - and a false sense of self-pride in our glorious past.

We are dead as people. Dying as a nation.

5

The Inverse Prism

Those who have loved are those that have found God
- Guru Nanak

"Have you been PERSONALLY harmed or put to inconvenience by any Muslim?" This friend posed the question when we met over dinner the other evening. For context only, he is a Hindu and had a right-leaning at some stage.

I thought for a few seconds. Early morning Azaan and offering Namaz by the roadside are no more inconvenient than a loudspeaker blaring Jagran songs all night, idols placed at road corners, or marriage processions blocking the traffic.

"Nope, on the contrary, I owe my existence to a kind Muslim family", I added. *"When my father was young, he was caught in the crossfire of pre-Independence communal riots in a Muslim-majority area. It was a kind Muslim gentleman who pulled him inside his house. And he stayed there till peace prevailed"*.

"That's precisely my point. I find your writings pretty balanced, but I have my friends who are constantly braying for blood on social media, writing and forwarding incendiary, hateful, spiteful messages, pictures and videos. And when I ask them, not one has come across a Muslim who has personally hurt him".

We moved on to other topics. But, I started reflecting on the psychology of these WhatsApp warriors. What motivates them to be so blind and vitriolic?

A person who never aspired to join the armed forces and loathes the idea of his children serving the nation at borders cries for open war with Pakistan to *"teach them a lesson"*. For all that you know, he has never met a Pakistani civilian.

Then, there are self-styled experts on international affairs, economics, constitution, and politics. Depending on their political affiliation, their views are invariably polarised, opinionated, and extreme. They will never consider others' points of view or enter into a conversation, an exchange, or a synthesis.

In a way, this entire CAA NRC debate has arisen precisely because of the lack of willingness of the ruling dispensation to engage and converse with different sections of society - intellectuals, opinion makers, journalists, and politicians on the side of the opposition. If it was done, the bill was referred to a select committee and allowed longer time for debates, discussion, and rallying around people; there could be less resistance. Why this tearing hurry? Why assume that everyone is out to break the nation and that the duty of serving the nation diligently lies only on your head that wears the crown of thorns?

The other disturbing aspect is to try to malign and character-assassinate anyone who takes a contrarian stand. Stand up with JNU students, and you are painted in black colour, called upon to boycott your movie and dug into the past of your family and friends...Why this anxiety to have everyone agree to your worldview?

A vibrant society should have all shades of opinion, and one should be able to take a stand without fear. There should be a civilised debate, explaining, listening, and agreeing to disagree politely. And there are no adverse consequences for your stand.

Only a vibrant, tolerant, free society can grow economically and be healthy and happy. Dissent is at the core of democracy, and any aberration should be handled with more democracy.

Two wrongs do not make one right. Just because we were wronged eight hundred years ago does not give us the right to seek revenge now.

A foreigner once asked me, "*What is quintessential Indian?*". I told him, "*The fact that there is nothing 'quintessential' is quintessentially Indian*".

Seriously, India is a kaleidoscope. The colour, sight, sound, and smell change every few km as if one is travelling on a train. It is a prism that splits white light into vibrant colours—each complete and beautiful yet complementing others.

Any attempt to invert the prism - that all shades of lights should become one white light as it passes through - and that light should be the only one and I and only I define it, is against our very grain as a nation-state, as a civilisation and as "*We, the people.*"

6

Happiness in Social Media

He who envies others does not obtain peace of mind
-Gautam Buddha

No sooner did the tourist bus start on the 'Cape of Good Hope' tour, than the percipient tour guide shared the bus Wi-Fi password with this vaticinal comment: "*Now that you have the password, you can safely ignore the beauty of nature and immerse yourself in the social media, to know how happy all your friends are, and how miserable your life is*". We all laughed at this rather acerbic, well-rehearsed joke.

Last week, on CNN, Farid Zakaria interviewed Prof. Sandra of Yale University, who specialises in human psychology.

She commented that, with increasing technology, the space for human-to-human communication is shrinking. We use ATMs to draw money, use ticket dispensers, buy groceries, do self-checkouts, etc. So, social media in its electronic form replaces the primaeval need for social interaction in a physical sense.

However, we do not discover the complete perspective or get to know all about our contacts on the social media. For example, most of us loathe to share uncomfortable, embarrassing, deeply personal, tragic, sorrowful, and emotional aspects of our lives—such as loneliness, ailments, fear, insecurities, prejudices, etc.

Your friends get to know only the pleasant parts of your life—your travels, success, promotions, etc.

It creates a feeling of '*I am the unlucky one. The rest of the world is happy.*'

The old culture of sitting with friends for endless hours, holding coffee mugs between palms, sometimes talking, at times falling silent, offering a touch of comfort, reading body language, sharing moments, sharing secrets, and shedding silent tears with your closest ones is out of fashion now.

We chase happiness by buying bigger apartments, maintaining comfortable spousal relationships, seeking a dramatic salary increase, and taking holidays in exotic places. But, we all know, these do not come quickly; hence, there is unhappiness as we look for instant gratification.

The Professor says that happiness comes from small things around us and is easy to achieve—a bright morning, the chirping of birds, children trotting about happily, sharing moments with friends over dinner, or interesting work at work.

We seem to be chasing the chimera but are oblivious that happiness lies around us, in small things that are easy and inexpensive to reach.

What a telling commentary on our society.

So, let me make a disclosure. I do share happy moments and visit places. But I also have my fair share of unhappiness, loneliness, and unfulfilled desires. I guess it is the same with each one of us.

That makes us human and fallible, making the need for physical, one-to-many interaction much more interesting and imperative. The digital world is just a supplement.

7

Substance Abuse

Every addiction is an attempt to slay hope
- Dan B Allender

It shall forever remain itched in my memory. Sitting cross-legged on a cement bench at a Dadar by lane was this middle-aged person, smoking through a tiny hole created at his neck (trachea)

A doctor friend explained later that this person might have undergone a surgical procedure called 'tracheostomy' to expose his windpipe for breathing, bypassing the God-given route—a possible case of cancer due to excessive smoking.

I only hope he lived long and could have improved his quality of life.

All around us, we see substance abuse - smoking, drinking, chewing tobacco, ganja, dependence on potent psychotropic substances...Humankind has found many ways to greet the creator early.

My reflection is that those who indulge in these (possibly, except for psychotropic substances) are doing it willingly, fully knowing the consequences and its impact on their family and their old age. There is no point taking refuse under statistical callisthenics, such as not every smoker dies early, and millions of non-smokers die prematurely every year.

So, why should society pay through public health expenditures for one's lifelong adventure? Make no mistake—even if one can afford private treatment, it does crowd out others (who might have been unlucky) and drive up prices due to the demand-supply balance. Besides, one's family pays for the inconvenience.

Should one not fund it now to create a corpus for old age debilitations? One way is to tax cigarettes and liquor heavily through a tax, tentatively named by me as 'Future Funding for Vices (FFV).' Invest these FFV into setting up care facilities for pulmonary diseases, liver-related ailments, and the dreaded 'C' word. Fund yourself and let public health support those who are sick - not due to their fault.

Extending logic further, those who take good care of themselves - regularly go to the gym, do yoga, and undertake periodic health checkups - should get tax benefits. Reward good and responsible citizens. If you cheat, well, you cannot cheat the nature. Can you?

The government has developed a new health policy, increasing health expenditures from 1.5% to 2.5% of GDP. It is time to innovate through a 'user pay' approach.

P.S. I saw disturbing news this morning that an upcoming model at Mysore, who was a drug addict, set her old grandparents' house on fire, locking them inside. They could luckily escape.

8
Linguistic Integration

To have another language is to possess a second soul.
- Charlemagne

Growing up in a small provincial town up east, far away from where your forefathers hailed, was very interesting. Not only did we have different names, eat 'exotic' meals, and celebrate different festivals (or festivals differently), but we also spoke a different language, with its script resembling *Jalebi* (An Indian sweetmeat in the shape of concentric circles and dipped in sugar syrup)

Most South Indians were either stenographers, nurses, IAS officers, or PSU employees on the 'Punishment' posting (as they thought, but most started liking the place and people soon). The prejudices, including our supposed fluency in English and our destiny of becoming IAS officers, were carried not only by fellow students but also by the teachers.

For all that you know, we were considered HSM - Homo Sapiens Madrasiens'.

Indian society may be patrilineal, but culture follows the matrilineal path. Since women had always come from the South, food and festivals were always celebrated the 'South Indian' way at home.

But it ended there. Our knowledge of South India was based entirely on movies shown on Doordarshan. So, in our 'imagined' world, a south Indian was either a highly cultured person with a delicate taste, was deeply religious and spoke in highly Sanskritized Telugu - or a kulak or a money lender, out to exploit the tribals and poor. We had the wisdom to discount as unreal the sword-wielding, wig-wearing king, giving a 10-minute, emotionally charged lecture, in black and white celluloid, on a battlefield.

In our 'imagined' world, a south Indian was a vegetarian, as most people around us were. It was shocking to know that the South had its own non-vegetarian 'delicacies' (oxymoronic as it may seem)

But, when it came to our mother tongue, we were - at best, 'Miscegenation,' at worst, linguistic vagabonds. Parents did apply soft pressure on girls to speak in their mother tongue (as they had to go to other families - hopefully back to where their forefathers came from), but boys were allowed to choose their lingua franca. Therefore, we were far more fluent in Hindi (and an illusion of English) than our mother tongue. Those coming fresh from the South were initially shocked at our linguistic choice. Some even took it as a lesson and forced (would even beat) their children to converse in their mother tongue. But, in due course, they all adopted local languages and dialects. Some married locally. Naturally, your dream girl or boy is someone you know, not someone living thousands of kilometres away. Isn't it?

In due course, even our parents mixed Hindi words in their Telugu and created a kind of pidgin. We were, after all, a cultural island!

And that is my reflection for today.

When I witness linguistic protests (the latest being signboards in three languages at the newly launched metro in Bangalore or bilingual passports), I want to reach out and tell the protestors that language cannot be imposed. Southern states' economic success attracts people from all over India who wish to contribute to and reap the benefits. Initially, they need help, such as signage, but they pick up local languages as time passes. Their children will think and speak in Telugu, Kannada, Tamil or Malayalam. They will read local literature. They will fall in love with their classmates and colleagues and marry them.

Sharp linguistic and cultural boundaries will diffuse whether we like it or not. The Internet, social media, affordable air travel, ease of relocation, and a more outgoing young generation will ensure this.

It is somewhat desirable, too. Did you realise that the next generation has risen above the demand for huge dowry by opting for a soulmate of their choice? In the process, they have solved an age-old disease. Many more evils and prejudices will disappear when people integrate and broaden their horizons.

Finally, each language is unique and beautiful. It needs to be promoted, respected, and preserved. A great way to do this is to create high-quality literature. You know a land and people by what they think and write.

I am learning Sanskrit because I aspire to read original texts. The investment in literature made by great scholars a couple of thousand years ago has ensured that Sanskrit lives within us.

9
Equality

When you meet Japanese people today, you are surprised by their humility. You could scarcely believe that two generations ago, their ancestors caused such global mayhem and brought untold misery upon so many nationalities.

Analyse how fiercely independent and votary of freedom an average white American is. Can you imagine that their forefathers indulged in the slave trade?

Australians are believed to have killed thousands of Aborigines in the most gruesome way - shooting them with nail guns.

Or did Europeans bring such misery and penury and kill the self-respect of their colonies?

You are witnessing the same with China today. Muscle flexing, sabre rattling, skirmishes—maybe war...

What connects all these? What is the underlying Least Common Multiple?

POWER. When you are in a position to dominate others, you get intoxicated. You forget the basic norms of good, humane behaviour. You dissociate yourself from your cultural moorings. You cease to be human beings.

Power corrupts—the ability to dominate blinds you.

Now, imagine, for most of Homo Sapiens history - around 60,000 years or more - men have dominated women. He was the breadwinner and protector. She was to sire the next generation and was the caregiver.

Imagine now, against the backdrop of my above examples, how much men have dominated women…We call it *Patriarchy.*

Of course, there have always been fair-minded people who treated women as equals. Many thought they were working for their emancipation (to me, this reeks of patriarchy—at least condescending). But overall, it was the men who dominated. Ever wonder how women could reach this far in claiming equality?

It was only in the last century or so that women started feeling equal. One main reason has been that most jobs now require skill (and not raw muscle) and a brain, and they are enabled by technology. Hence, men have no natural physical advantage over women. Women claim their rightful place from the laboratory to war, the cricket field to the classroom.

Now, peep into the future, when technology will fundamentally alter how we interact with others and our surroundings. Experts tell us we are just at the beginning of the age of machines.

And machines are gender-neutral. Will our sex matter at all, then? Will women be truly equal to men, then?

Shall we remain viviparous? Or, as Aldous Huxley wrote in 1929 in his masterpiece '*The Brave New World*', shall we only manufacture babies in test tubes? The oviparous way shall advent? Batches, whose chemical combination will be altered to suit the needs of society then?

Will gender matter? Or even equality, for that matter? Or even emotions? Will we be less violent through chemical manipulation of our building blocks?

10
Gutter Cleaning

India will have to hang down her head in shame if even one person is left who is said in any way to be untouchable.
- Lal Bahadur Shastri

A video showing a young boy touching the cheek of his dead father at a morgue and breaking down, crying 'Papa' has gone viral in India.

The young person in the video died due to asphyxiation and toxic gas while cleaning a sewer. He belonged to the lower caste, as it usually happens in India.

The still picture, mercifully masked, broke one's heart. I could not bring myself to watch the video.

A family stood devastated as the sole breadwinner was cruelly snatched away due to workplace danger. And with that, the future of the young lad...

But India stood in unison. Over Rs five million was collected through donations. Indeed, it cannot compensate for the loss of a father or a husband, but it can mitigate their hardship.

It gives one solace that we Indians have our hearts in the right place. Despite being loud, emotional, and breaking into road rage, we still care for those in need. A case in point is the donations we give liberally after natural disasters.

But do our employers, administrators, contractors, and politicians have any heart? Or are they only a selfish blood-pumping mechanism?

How else would you explain such apathy, incidence after incidence and compromise on workplace safety?

Cleaning sewers is the worst kind of employment one can dream of. However, I have not heard of workers choking and dying in developed nations or the Middle East. Indeed, they take adequate precautions, provide masks, and use machines for this task.

Why can't we? Why could the young man not be trained to use machines to clean sewers? No one is untrainable.

Carrying night soil was banned in India decades ago. But, in smaller places, in my childhood, pit toilets and the practice of carrying night soil continued for decades. We were lucky to have modern toilets. And trust me, the word 'untouchable' assumes a new meaning - it just personifies the practice. Remember that famous Satyajit Ray movie - *Sadgati*..

Better workplace facilities bring disproportionate benefits. I read somewhere that eye tests and glasses among tea garden workers increased productivity by 33%.

Why can we not be more humane? Why can we not adopt better safety standards? Why can we not adopt modern means, especially in hazardous operations? Or for socially degrading professions? Why do we exploit the helpless?

It needs us to be human. Which, the powerful are not ..

That is the tragedy - and a helpless reality.

11

Cognitive Constructs

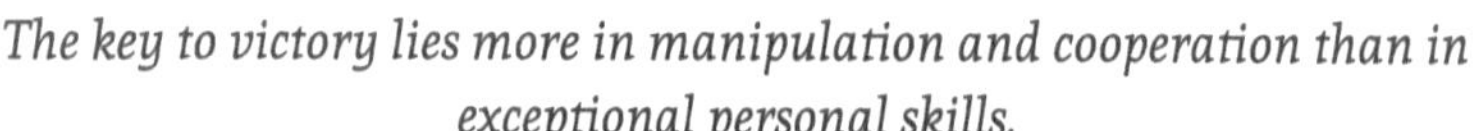

The key to victory lies more in manipulation and cooperation than in exceptional personal skills.
- Yuval Noah Harari

I read a fascinating book (*A Brief History of Mankind* - Author - Yuval Noah Harari) on the evolution of Homo Sapiens (literally meaning 'wise man' in Latin) - one of the many books I have read on this rather intriguing topic, which borders science and conjectures.

The author argues that what sets Homo Sapiens apart is our cognitive abilities. We broke away from other animals, including primate cousins, when we experienced a cognitive revolution.

Now, what is this concept?

Animals have been able to live in groups (family, territorial bands, etc.) for over a millennium. And they needed communication and support. For example, they alert each other about a lion sighting near the waterhole. It was a collective good that forced animals to communicate with each other and create bonds.

However, animals can't be in constant touch with each other once the group size exceeds a few dozen—perhaps a hundred or so. Then, the group has to break up and explore new niches.

As against the 'fact' of sighting a lion, the 'belief' that a spirit in the grove needs to be propitiated lest it harms the group required the power to 'imagine'. This belief-based construct, rather than fact-based communication, sets Homo Sapiens apart. This is the cognitive revolution.

It is this ability to create beliefs that made homo sapiens appeal to higher but abstract collective goals—and made it possible to create God, religion, etc. It made it possible for large groups to come together and build civilisation. Even though they hardly met all the others, they all believed in common abstract goals.

Why did this cognitive revolution happen? I suspect homo sapiens always felt the pangs of separation. It desired to keep the flock together, growing and securing one another. Even today, the marriage of children, heartbreak, family breakups, separation of employees and parting with clods of land are painful events.

Is nationalism also a common abstraction? What changes when I set my feet on the other side of the national border? Nothing in terms of geography, flora, fauna, language, food, people, etc. Yet, the entire attitude changes. So powerful is this abstraction.

Human beings have been migratory since time immemorial. From the proverbial African Eve, somewhere in present-day Kenya, we have moved to all parts of the earth (and beyond). Yet nationalism puts artificial restrictions (and formal procedures) on human movement. We are prepared to pay an inhuman cost to zealously protect our boundaries, our culture, our way of life, and our economy. Mark carefully—each of the above is a cognitive abstraction.

That explains why nation-states keep invoking patriotism and sometimes strident nationalism. It helps the flock unite and sacrifice the current for an assumed future. Liberal minds harp on peaceful co-existence, forgiveness, inclusiveness, etc.

These are battles of ideas.

12
Scientific Revolution

Our scientific power has outrun our spiritual power. We have guided missiles and misguided men.
- Martin Luther King, Jr.

This excellent book, Sapiens—*A Brief History of Mankind* (Author - Yuval Noah Harari), argues that the world we see today resulted from several revolutions. The cognitive revolution was the beginning, about which I alluded to in one of my earlier writings.

The author argues that the world was the same between 1000 AD and 1500 AD. However, around 1500 AD, a revolution occurred in hitherto unknown Europe. We call it the scientific revolution.

Curiosity and an unwillingness to accept gospel truth were at the very base of this revolution. We also needed to admit that we knew little about other parts of the earth, natural phenomena, and our bodies.

This eagerness to explore and to know through experiments, coupled with funding (capitalism), an independent judiciary, and political sagacity, transformed humanity over the next few hundred years, which made Europeans rule the world. Of course, it had its adverse consequences, such as slavery, bitter wars, subjugation, and genocide.

What is important is that investment in science created the bedrock on which the technological revolution, followed by the information revolution, is based.

It underpins the importance of investing in science. Observe closely—superpowers and emerging superpowers like China have invested heavily in education, especially in the sciences. That is the key to growth and claiming one's rightful place worldwide.

Therefore, when I read about the Facebook post by one of our senior Physics Professor and an admirable teacher), that at my University, there is a lack of teachers, academics are suffering, research quality has gone down and passing examinations is the main aim, and prestigious courses are not being filled, I felt very sad.

Around us, too, I see students opting for technology courses, as they assure jobs, unlike pure sciences (which they cannot be faulted for). The overall rigour in technology education has also gone down. Teachers are disinterested, and students look for an easy way out. When they enter the corporate world, employers must invest in re-educating them.

Unless we understand that India needs targeted, relevant, and high-quality skill sets to attract some of the best brains in fundamental scientific research, we will continue to be laggards. We will not reach our potential and reclaim our supposed past glory.

Do we have it in our leaders to understand and address this?

13
A Brave New World

<hr>

Technological progress has merely provided us with more efficient means for going backwards.
- Aldous Huxley

In his brilliant satirical novel '*A Brave New World*', written in the nineteen twenties, Aldous Huxley conceptualises a world where human children are neither viviparous (born out of the womb) nor oviparous (born out of an egg). Instead, children are created in batches by combining sperm and egg and hatching it in a tube for nine months. Along the way, chemical processes are adopted to alter building blocks to create children with different abilities. So, you have batches of Alpha Plus (the thinkers, scientists, etc.) to Delta (menial workers). They are rewarded differently, and Delta gets part of the payment as *sura* (intoxicant).

The rationale was that society needed people with different skill sets, and forced adoption to work in a way not suited for one's genetic predisposition would lead to dissatisfaction and would pull down the brave New World.

Not that the biological needs of sex were alien in this world. It is purely physiological, devoid of emotions and the functional purpose of procreation.

In this brave new world, an alien from the old world arrives and falls genuinely and madly in love with a pretty damsel, who, of course, has no feelings of any kind. All hell breaks loose.

Controlling people's minds is as old as the institution of democracy, whether it was rabble-rousing or demagoguery—from Hitler to Indira Gandhi (remember, the original Jumla—*Garibi Hatao* (banish poverty).

Stratification and appeal to people's differential needs seem to be byproducts of democracy simply because there was never enough to give everyone what they needed.

Thus came pandering to the expectations of a narrow group of people—the voters. The guardians of democracy sought to appeal to and pander to the numerically large and influential segments of society. Yet others looked at creating a loyal set of voters by pandering to the fear of smaller segments. So, you had schisms of caste, religion, levels of prosperity, pro or anti-gun lobby etc., etc.

India also witnessed attempts to widen the existing schism - accentuate the divide - to be used during hustings. Caste riots, crass appeals, and incendiary statements were all designed for it.

As social media gained popularity, an inexpensive way was found to use the existing support base to spread motivated messages. Just observe how many politically loaded messages you receive. And it comes from your friends, who unwittingly act as vectors of fake news, crass jokes, lampooning cartoons, and dividing messages.

Now, we are entering the next phase, whereby an attempt is made to influence your thinking by seeping into your mind. As the CEO of Cambridge Analytica revealed, "to inject into the bloodstream of subjects". It entails analysing your behaviour through social profiling and social media behaviour (your friends, your likes, choice of words, purchases, reading, demographic details) and subtly giving you messages to alter your viewpoint. Mass data analysis is carried out to find which message should target you, how and when.

Scary? No. It is just a progression of our evolution as social animals. If not CA, someone else will do it. It may be even more covert. After all, we have the tools (analytics) and understanding of the human psyche (behavioural psychology), plus the means of rapid dissemination of mass customised trash.

You may think you are different. Most will fall for it.

No, we did not create babies in tubes by altering their DNA using biology and chemistry. Instead, we are seeking to change minds and behaviours through psychology.

That will be a fitting tribute to Huxley, as his book celebrates its centenary in less than ten years.

14
Being Good

Thousands of candles can be lit from a single candle, and the life of the candle will not be shortened. Happiness never decreases by being shared.
- Gautama Buddha

During a conversation with Prophet Mohammed (Peace be upon him), a person referred to someone else as a *'good person'*

The Prophet asked him, "*How do you know? Did you travel with him? Did he share his bread and water with you?*"

Travel in those days, especially in the deserts of Arabia, was arduous. Everything was in short supply. And one had to be generous, empathetic, and large-hearted to share scarce lifesaving food and other precious resources with others.

If the Prophet were to converse today, he would have asked, "*Well, how do you know? Did he make way for others at the crowded hospital?*"

During the last two days, I spent a good part of my time at a major hospital's outpatient department (OPD).

There is a scene of crying humanity in the basement section. Worried faces about themselves or their loved ones, cranky children, those unable to read signboards and walking confused, people of all economic statuses from different parts of India and neighbouring countries crowding around doctors' cabins, diagnostic labs, medical counters, and billing counters. That long Aaah, while taking out crumpled notes from the pocket of a soiled shirt.

My problems were much less, but I did have my uncertainties. Well, no health problem is minor. If at all, it is on a relative scale. It seems minor when you see children, the elderly, the emaciated, the physically challenged, etc., and further observe mothers with moist eyes and hands joined in prayer all around you.

External stimuli added to my peevishness. I had braved peak Bangalore traffic for well over an hour and a half on a pothole-ridden road, only to find no vacant parking slot at the hospital and was forced to pay usurious premium parking charges.

I am sure we all have seen this and worse. After all, none among us was born as Gautama, protected by a doting father, King Shuddhodhan.

Did it ever occur to you that in the midst of all these, someone... some random person radiates a smile at you? The reassuring one, the one of hope and understanding?

Or someone lightly touches you on your shoulder, strikes up a small conversation, and tells you that things would brighten up?

Or someone who accosts the sister on duty and leaves a quiet message to attend to someone who seemed in greater and urgent need of attention and that he would be okay to wait longer?

Or does someone tell the patient in crutches at the medical counter to jump the queue ahead of her?

In short, that 'good one' who radiates warmth, spreads hope, puts others ahead of narrow self and brightens up your day and the ill-lit basement of the hospital?

Well, trust me, it happens. And that makes life so much more bearable.

Our life is like a train journey from childhood, which we fondly recall. We share the cabin with strangers and soon introduce ourselves. Children start playing with their kids, and we share food, converse, crack jokes, and care for each other's belongings.

When you reach your destination, the co-passengers help you offload your luggage. You exchange addresses, promise to be in touch, and children hug each other.

As the train leaves, you wave feverishly till the passengers' palms disappear into the window.

You march towards the exit. You know you shall never meet again or even converse. Yet, you have spring in your stride, lightness in your heart, and honey-like sweetness on your lips, notwithstanding the travails of a long journey—heat, dirt, and noise around you.

And you know what is goodness around you. Be it the desert journey, hospital, train travel, or life itself.

Can we strive to be that good one?

15
Me Too

There is no kind of harassment that a man may not inflict on a woman with impunity in civilised societies.
- Denis Diderot

During a drive between Sringeri and Chikmagalur on a highway cutting through lush green fields, we slowed down to make way for a bunch of girls, huddled in small groups, returning home at the end of school hours. Three teenage boys riding a bike, without wearing helmets, drove past them, veering close to them, making some gestures, and I guess, some lewd comments. The startled & terrified girls were pushed literally to the edge of the road to avoid being run over.

I am sure this is not an isolated incidence deep inside rural India.

'Boys will be boys', did you hear the patriarch say? Someone who knew the pulse of the rural north too well?

Do you think 'Me Too' was purely an urban phenomenon, restricted to the high and mighty, socialites, educated, visible public figures from media, films, and some top-notch institutions?

Let us face it. Bullying, harassment, sexual innuendo, exploitation from a position of dominance, and violation happen in every walk of life. It is not restricted to women. Transgender people have been facing it in a crass and obscene way for the most prolonged period in our country. Children, too, face it. And some men face it too, though more often in domestic situations.

The problem is not with men. The problem lies with our deeply entrenched patriarchal society, where the sense of entitlement and 'getting away with it' has seeped in. Giving a job to someone is not a recognition of one's skill sets and for receiving productive output, but a favour meted out to someone. Our patriarchy ensures indifference to the sensitivity of others, oblivious to violations, as much as refusal to move ahead with times. Some remain steeped in the imagined past, though I doubt if the glorious past tolerated such indifference and violations.

As the skeletons started tumbling out, the high and mighty stand exposed. I believe the natural and logical end shall be through due judicial process. A fair and sensitive trial, due process of law, witnesses, cross-examination, and evaluation of evidence should ensure proper justice. Even in prominent and extreme cases, including rape in a position of dominance, and physical and mental abuse, the judicial approach remains the best bet.

However, the law has been strengthened only after the Vishakha judgement in the nineties and the recent Nirbhaya Act, making sexual violence much broader in scope. Hundreds of cases predate these, and laws cannot be applied retrospectively. More importantly, in many cases, violations happen in seclusion, and every possible case of a breach cannot be covered under the penal code.

It is sufficient if a woman feels violated. She has a right to remedial action, redressal, and assurance of safety in the future.

I believe 'Me Too' serves its purpose precisely when the law seems imbecile, and naming and shaming remain the only deterrent. But this, too, has its limitations.

First, the cost of violation is high only for those in public life who have much to lose. What about the small fries who perpetrate it away from the glare of the media, like the female janitorial help at the hands of the contractual supervisor?

Secondly, it risks running out of steam and making the patriarchs get back with a vengeance—defamation, boycott, causing injury to insult.

Thirdly, the real big ones - the industry's flagpoles would possibly never be exposed, given their influence, the respect they command, their sheet presence and the fear factor. No one would dare to do so

Finally, one vengeful false case of 'Me Too' is enough to discredit the entire social movement.

My submission is that while 'Me Too' is an excellent initiative, it needs to be supplemented with a broader movement, for example, against films that are full of double entendre and suggestive dialogue, patriarchal stereotypes, advertisements that depict stereotypes, and serials that strengthen the patriarchy in the name of tradition.

The movement must go beyond TV studios and social media to public places, parks, malls, schools and offices. And extend to social and economic boycotts.

Silence in the face of a violation of dignity is complicity and provides oxygen to the violators.

I am very proud of the fact that the organisation that I co-founded has faced practically no violation of dignity. 'Practically no', as I am unsure if my colleagues' actions at some stage or other gave an impression of being patriarchal and condescending. We, too, are products of the same patriarchal order. We treat employees as colleagues (and not as family members!), and they work with us with dignity to earn, learn and shape their future. And we have proclaimed ZERO tolerance in aberrant cases.

What should one do if faced with a violation? One should adopt the following.

1) *Protest* at the first sign of such an attempt. Make it clear you are not amused and will not tolerate it. Confront if you feel even slightly violated. A tight slap, if you think it right. A stitch in time saves nine.

2) *Report* to the right persons. For minor indiscretions, could you let HR know?

3) *Inform* others. Let your colleagues, including male colleagues, know and encourage them to observe and confirm if needed

4) *Complain* formally. Organisations have compliance committees and POSH (Prevention of Sexual Harassment)

committees. Could you take formal action?

5) *Escalate.* If you are not heard, if violations continue, do take the matter up at the highest level and with the Police and women's commission.

In short, PRICE. That is the acronym for the five points I mentioned above.

This is the price we pay for our dignity. As my mother says, do not seek even the kingdom of heaven at the cost of dignity.

An equal society can be built only when it is fair, equitable, fearless, provides equal opportunity and ensures freedom and security. Individual dignity is the bedrock of the society that we all wish to create.

16
millets

So, millets are the new-found wonder food and the flavour of the day.

Yes, the same coarse, hardy grains that could survive arid conditions were grown in plenty all over India before the green revolution emphasised producing wheat and rice. Our forefathers knew these as jowar, bajra, ragi, etc.; village folks and those less fortunate consumed them.

We are now told that millet is incredibly healthy as it is low in gluten and carbohydrates. No wonder socialites visit organic shops draped in hard starched cotton saris, wearing coin-sized bindis and playing marble-sized bead necklaces to buy pearl millet, small millet, horse millet, etc.

It is a revivalism of some sort. The old order is returning as we have rediscovered ancient wisdom.

We were scoffed at for using salt and charcoal to brush teeth or, for that matter, clove oil to fight toothache. However, clove oil is making a comeback in toothpaste.

From modern medicines, we are rediscovering the magic of ancient medicines.

Instead of visiting noisy and smelly gymnasiums, yoga, Pranayam, and meditation are known and practised.

What our forefathers used to nourish the plants and drive away pests is now being hailed as organic farming, which commands a premium.

And the crowning glory is that we are now being educated that Indian squat toilets are better designed than the WC (aka Italian ones). I am not sure how many, in their privacy, are placing a stool under their feet, hoping to metamorphose from *Piku's* baba (Protagonist in a popular Indian movie, in which a young girl takes care of her choleric and chronically constipated old father) to the sentry of the museum at Mr. Beans (The movie in which Mr Beans mixes up keys of the toilet at the museum).

At this rate, the West will rediscover that our sages lived on tubers and raw food and were healthier.

Who knows, we may have McTuber one day, and at a swanky office, one could open a tiffin box to eat boiled shakarkand!

17

Waiting Upon You

The function of freedom is to free someone else.
-Toni Morrison

As I venture out for my post-dinner stroll, I see our building security staff sit down for dinner at the security cabin. I complete my stroll and go back to retire to my cosy bed. They prepare to guard us from all imaginary attacks - from attempted larceny to lethal biological weapons. Armed with a bamboo stick and a whistle, assisted by a tall gate, barbed wire atop an imposing boundary wall and a few floodlights.

I did not start observing him until I was nominated to one of the committees in our residential complex, except when we were distributing sweets during Diwali or gifting earthen water pots just before the onset of summer. Our motive was purely selfish - to feel better after doing something for less-endowed people.

He still stands there. Could you look out of your window? He is standing there, opening and closing the gate, enquiring with the visitors, entering details in the visitor's register, etc.

Most of the chaps come from the impoverished eastern part of shanty towns and earn a very meagre income. They migrate to big cities to keep their body and soul together and to shield themselves from coming in harm's way in insurgency-ridden states.

Do you know how much he earns? Typically, Rs 5000 per month. He works 12 hours a day, 7 days a week, 52 weeks a year. Of course,

"

on paper, his employer makes him sign that he works for 8 hours and gets a week off. The officials are blind—just like the justice system.

He works more than 12 hours continuously. When the shift changes (day to night), he works for 24 continuous hours. If the reliever runs away or does not turn up, it could stretch up to 36 or even 48 hours. He sits in that small box at your gate and sometimes wanders around the perimeter.

It is a thankless job. If they fall asleep at night (I thought God made night to sleep, no?), they suffer a hefty deduction from their subsistence allowances. Regarding job satisfaction, they are just below call centre personnel, which is how most residents and visitors deal with them.

How does he live and run his family? He pays a bribe for a ration card and stands in the queue to get his share of the ration. He shares a dingy with some 12 others, where water needs to be purchased, as there is no running water (did you shout at him for opening the garden tap the other day?). He is picked up at the shanty and dropped off at your doorstep by the contractor. And because he is expected to look bright and alert, he wears a crisp uniform, a (shared) tie, and a pair of shoes. It does not matter if his stomach is empty. It is better if he is hungry. He could doze off, otherwise jeopardising your security.

One day, someone complained that they were not well-groomed, their shoes were not shining, and their uniforms were not pressed. I retorted that for the salary we pay them, surely we did not expect the Commissioner of Police to guard us personally.

He has to save something from this Rs 5,000. There are hungry mouths to be fed and sisters to be married off in some remote villages.

And, yes, he gets beaten up, too. Sometimes, it's by the contractor (who can proudly tell you he has disciplined him) and sometimes by your fellow apartment owners or visitors. Who is he to ask for a vehicle pass? He's a worthless fellow. Getting shouted at is part of his occupational risk, anyway.

In my complex, a contractor snatched away one of the guards' golden chain (his only possession, gifted by his mother) after somebody complained about the loss of some junk water pump. (Why should people with low incomes wear a gold chain in the first place?).

Yet, he too is the apple of somebody's eye (yes, poor too can be the darling of his parents!). He comes from Assam, North East, Bihar, Orissa etc. Not necessarily due to appalling poverty. But, more often, it was to protect him from the ULFAs of the world (ULFA was a militant organisation in North East of India. Young are especially vulnerable to forced induction into one of the militant outfits, and the only way to save them, in many places, is to send them to Bangalore or Gurgaon. Parents will somehow manage!! Talk about law and order and Mera Bharat Mahaan.

That is precisely my reflection for the day. We are a very unequal society (all societies are - degrees may differ), where upward mobility and recognition are ascribed rather than achieved. Accident of birth determines if greatness is thrust upon you (as happens all around us) or you are condemned to eke out a living and have no social security umbrella upon your head, with very few exceptions, which are inspirational stories. Yes, stories are suitable for bedtime reading, not to be lived through, for the vast multitude.

What can you do for him?

Firstly, treat him as a human being. He is just following your instructions and does not deserve your anger.

Secondly, could you make sure that his contractor deals with him fairly? This means creating a buffer and negotiating shorter working hours, etc. Your maintenance charges could go up, but be humane.

Lastly, please see if you can help him. Some may have sick people behind them, and some want to complete their education. Help him individually and collectively.

He deserves it. It could be you, but for the providence of your birth!

45

18
Rickshaw Puller

All work is noble; the only ignoble thing is to live without working.
- Maria Montessori

I am unsure how many of you have taken a ride on a cycle rickshaw—not the motorised one! Those who hail from small towns would indeed have.

The non-motorized one comes in two varieties. The hand-pulled one, then mostly seen in Calcutta by lanes (yes, it was Calcutta in my growing-up days), so immortalised in the epic Balraj Sahni movie 'Do Bigha Jameen' (Small parcel of land). The travails of a rickshaw puller who makes every effort to get back his land from the money lender. And, finally, he fails to get even a clod of land.

I never had the stone heart or courage to hop onto one of the hand-pulled rickshaws.

But things were different when it came to the pedal rickshaw. In small towns, if you did not own a vehicle, it was the principal mode of transport. It still is—and it is gratifying that battery-powered ones in many small places are replacing it.

Travel by rickshaw was always a pleasant experience. Walking through town traffic, one could get a slow 360-degree view of the surroundings, read name boards, observe people and distant objects come closer, walk by you in reverse, and then fade behind you. If the rickshaw puller were in a good mood, he would chat with you or even hum a song or two.

The idyllic setting described above ends there. It is a very, very demanding job. I have observed it at close quarters. A few rickshaw pullers in my provincial town would keep their rickshaws in our compound. Some would keep their savings with us and collect them back when visiting home. Most were displaced labourers or landless poor. Circumstances drove some. Some were on weed (or something local but intoxicating). Some would be professional blood donors.

Most rickshaw pullers did not own rickshaws. They took it in daily hire from the 'rickshaw kings'. It was common to overload and struggle to pull the vehicle to maximise their earnings.

As a kid, my heart went out to the rickshaw puller, who was exposed to the elements, had meagre conveniences, and lived on a frugal diet. How could one survive this way?

Come to think of it; you feel how lucky you are to have a comfortable upbringing and life overall (sure, lots and lots of parental sacrifice and toil went into making our lives comfortable). On the other hand, you observe, at close quarters, the lives of those who are underprivileged and live at the margin of society.

Would the world ever be a fair place?

19
Child Domestic Servant

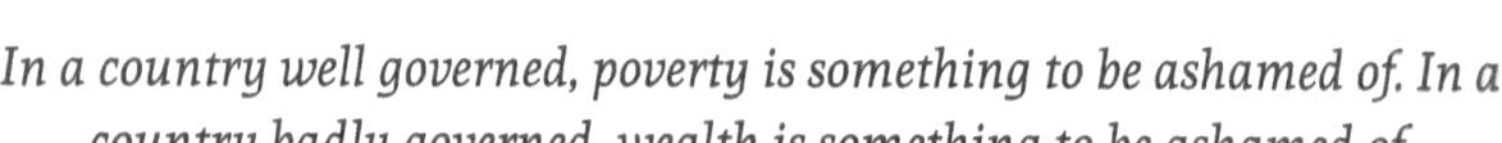

In a country well governed, poverty is something to be ashamed of. In a country badly governed, wealth is something to be ashamed of.
- Confucius

You have possibly not missed her. At the shopping mall, carrying a toddler not much younger than her, following the memsahib. Please take a look carefully next time. Her inescapable blank gaze was nothing to cheer about today, or for that matter, nothing to look forward to in future.

You see her everywhere—in plush shopping arcades, manicured parks, railway stations, your gated community, and, sometimes, the airport. Occasionally, it is Pappu, not Rani.

Make no mistake—this ten-year-old is very useful and inexpensive. Plucked from her nursery in Jharkhand, she works 16 hours daily—from minding the child to cleaning the house, washing clothes, and running errands. She lives in someone's balcony and subsists on frugal food and used clothes. Possibly, she has been lulled into a bright future in the city, where she will get a chance to go to school and shape her future. Welcome to modern-day slavery.

I often wonder why it has to be a young girl who has to take care of kids; why not someone in her twenties or thirties? Why rob a child of her childhood?

I know. You are going to say that she is at least getting two square meals and shelter and is not being abused. (I'm not so sure. Possibly, she is disciplined once in a while within the confines of the house. Did you care to see if her tears had dried up in her cheek? Did you ever try to hear a muffled cry emanating from the other side of your wall?).

Come on, madam. If you cared, you would have sponsored her education and given her a future, and she would undoubtedly be carrying her own a decade from now, not your kid.

Ironically, the memsahib and sahib rejoice when Kailash Satyarthi gets a noble, discusses women's liberty over cappuccino at Starbucks, recently celebrated women's day at the office and took out a candlelight procession on social issues.

I reflect that you do not need to go far to see abuse and violence. It is around you - when you amble across the park, within your residential blocks, and, at times, your home. Violence is within.

Except it lurks under the veneer of your epidermis. You have chosen to be a pachyderm.

20

Old age and Support

In youth, the days are short and the years are long. In old age, the years are short and days long.
- Pope Paul VI

A rather poignant picture went viral some time back. This 2007 picture, shot by a BBC photojournalist in Gujarat, depicted a young schoolgirl visiting a nursing home and finding her grandmother admitted there. She was told that her grandmother was visiting relatives. The weeping grandmother in embrace with her loving but helpless granddaughter attracted lots of attention.

I was talking about this to a few friends - happily, all of them take good care of their parents - but each one believed they should end their last few years in some retirement home (a euphemism for a nursing home).

As someone who has lived nearly all his life with his parents and received their love, affection, advice, wisdom, and companionship, I was forced to reflect. Are we progressing or regressing?

As a believer in my religion, I am amazed at the ancient wisdom, self-abnegation and living in harmony with nature. However, the Ashram system left me a little puzzled.

The ashram system consists of four states of life—Brahmacharya, Grihastha, Vanaprastha, and Sanyas - roughly a quarter of the average lifespan.

Another variant, which is commonly believed in the South (and that explains symbolic remarriage at age 60 called Shasti purti), is that lifespan is divided into the first twelve years of learning at home, then twelve years of formal education at Gurukul, followed by twenty-four years of Grihastha, then twelve years of living separately - understanding and preparing for renunciation - symbolic remarriage at sixty - to quench the fire of spirit, not of the body - then from age sixty to seventy-two taking care of each other, but away from children and then complete renunciation at age 72 and wander into the forest, waiting for salvation.

Either interpretation leads to only one conclusion. As per the scriptures, you must fend for yourself in your old age. When you need them most, when you are emasculated, emaciated, and diseased, your children are not with you.

I find it unacceptable.

There is no greater pleasure than having the company of family elders among you. They are always there to guide you, participate in your life, enrich you, and help you remain connected with your roots.

I pity those who do not have the good luck of being with family elders. I also feel sorry for those who leave their precious family members in a nursing home.

I thought this happened only among Eskimos and hunter-gatherers. The harshness of existence made it imperative not to be impeded by the old and sick - pure social biology.

Not for us, who live in comfort and luxury and are well provided for by nature, the economy, sciences, technology, and society.

21

Vitriol in Social Media

Social media is both a dark and brilliant thing for mental health.
- Fearne Cotton

I have stopped watching news channels for a few months now, and I am much more at ease with myself and my surroundings. Plus, I am spared the opprobrious high-pitched debates, opinionated masquerading as experts, and divisive narratives. I use my TV to watch sports, information, and, occasionally, movies.

It's not that I am not up to date on the news. I check it on news portals and can afford to be selective in what (and who) I want to read.

For several months now, I have been contemplating leaving social media altogether. But that would make me very lonely. Facebook and WhatsApp are the new-age living rooms. I talk to my friends and make new and valuable connections here.

And that is precisely the point. I do not always engage in heated, vitriolic debates in my living room. Why do we do it on social media?

It is like driving. A perfectly gentle person becomes irascible once behind the wheel. Every car ahead of you is an impediment, every pedestrian is an imbecile, and every red signal conspires against you.

Like you all, I receive a lot of forwards containing incendiary messages, splenetic rants, photoshopped images, morphed videos, polarising political views, gratuitous comments, half-baked medical advice, and ribald jokes. Most do not originate from my friends, but I am occasionally guilty of association through forwarding them.

And some conversations are equally rancorous. How can people live with so much bile in their system?

If one looks closely, most searing debates are about politics and religion. These are immensely debatable but in an agreeable, dignified way.

The scriptures say

Satyam Bruyat, Priyam Bruyat, Na Bruyat, SatyamAPriyam

[*Speak the truth, speak with affection and love, and do not speak the truth that hurts.*]

I am also reminded of

Raja Swadeshe Pujyate, Vidwan Sarvatra Pujyate

[*A king is respected in his land, but a scholar is universally acclaimed.*]

Why not debate in a scholarly way? For a long time, I have been convinced that our hope of governments and political entities being agents and catalysts for socio-economic changes is highly exaggerated. If one wants to bring change, do it yourself. My trust in the next generation is more than mine in the administration. So, why waste time and energy on political debates?

Finally, the scriptures say

Ekam SadViprah bahudha Vadanti AgniM YamM Matarishvanamahuh

[*The truth is, scholars say, that one can reach it through various means.*]

We belong to such a wholehearted, broad-minded religion.

Do we need to be so regressive, so spiteful of other people's religious beliefs and proclivities?

22
Retirement Planning

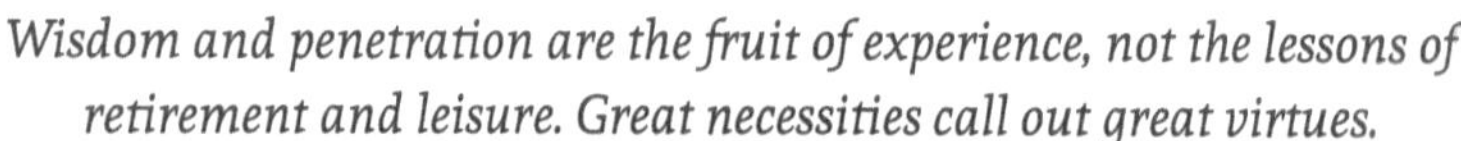

Wisdom and penetration are the fruit of experience, not the lessons of retirement and leisure. Great necessities call out great virtues.
- Abigail Adams

A close relative of mine is busier after retirement than he was during regular employment. He developed some niche skills towards the end of his career, developed a passion for IT systems, and immersed himself in training, skill development and consulting immediately after his retirement. Retirement has not changed his lifestyle a bit.

On the other hand, I know of people who treat their retirement as an unexpected and rude shock. How to keep themselves busy and make up for the loss of income draws them down, sometimes even into depression. Suddenly, you find them looking old and bent, lacking self-confidence, feeling unwanted even in the family, and being irascible. Some even die prematurely—prematurely because the early sixties is no age to die.

Why this polar opposite reaction? Indeed, one knows about the date of one's retirement (unless involuntary), the consequences on financial security, and the availability of time after retirement.

This has to do with the preparation one does in life, well in time.

Retirement is a milestone in life, like marriage, childbirth, and children's marriage. It does not signal the end of one's shelf life. Human beings do not expire, unlike medicines.

Of course, not everyone is fortunate enough, and one size does not fit all. At this stage of life, one may have suffered the loss of a spouse, lived in an empty nest, experienced ill health of self or near and dear, lost lifelong friends, or dealt with unfortunate cases of uncaring family. Some might not have enough savings due to high expenses, especially on education and health in earlier days. Unfortunately, this world is unfair and does not do equal justice to all. God may be kinder to some.

I submit that these are life-stage-dependent situations, not precipitated by retirement.

Trust me, lots of anxieties lie in the mind. You are not obligated to earn till your last breath. You are a human being, not a note-printing machine. You, too, have only one life. Well, you may have a rebirth if you are a Hindu or a Buddhist, but you have no divine guarantee of a human form. So, relax.

Unless one needs financial support, one should not look for paying jobs. One should start a new inning and chase dreams and avocation. Leave the job market for those who need it, including the next generation. Typically, your expenses reduce drastically after retirement.

One should contribute to society through one's lifelong acquired skill sets. Get involved in education, health, and cleanliness—there is so much to do around you. A pair of hands that joins to serve is dearer to God than the one that rises to pray.

Do take care of your health. Healthy habits need to be inculcated early in life, but following an active and engaged life can ameliorate later suffering to a good extent. There is no substitute for decent medical insurance.

You can plan your financial security early. Even small savings early in life lead to a significant corpus later. Invest judiciously. Financial security gives self-confidence.

Invest in relationships and stay engaged, even through social media. These give life purpose and make it richer.

Drop all regrets and bickering in life. Like Sunil Gavaskar, after completing a century, take a fresh guard and start with a score of zero again.

What you get is God's gift to you. What you become is your Gift to God.

23

Homeopathy

*By concentrating on smaller and smaller fragments of the body –
shifting its perspective from the study of bodily organs and their
functions to that of cells and, finally, to the study of molecules – modern
medicine often loses sight of the human being and has reduced health to
mechanical functioning.*
- Fritjof Capra

Having observed Homeopathy and Homeopathic doctors for nearly all my adult life, I am convinced that homoeopathy is beneficial. I have seen unbelievable results in seemingly hopeless situations. Therefore, I disagree with those who call homoeopathy a 'faith' medicine or a placebo. Faith is necessary for any medicine to work, I am convinced.

However, I have lots of problems with homoeopathic doctors, especially the big names. Consider this

1) Most big doctors make it very difficult to get an appointment. For example, asking patients to drop a postcard only to get an appointment several months later, asking patients to arrive at 4 a.m. to collect the token, etc. Check the famous names in eastern India. Fortunately, the new generation of doctors is more approachable.

2) I often wonder if all the information they collect during case-taking is useful. Whether I put my left leg first in my pyjamas has any bearing to understanding me holistically!

3) Homeopathic doctors criticise other medicines, including other homoeopaths, with a few exceptions. You come back, wondering if all the months and years of your treatment were worthless.

4) Their claims of results are anecdotal and without any scientific rigour. So, it is left to you to believe them. Coupled with the fact that for the same symptoms, different medicines are prescribed for other patients and lots of hits and trial is done on the same patient, you are gambling in some way if you have reposed your faith in Homeopathy.

5) Homeopaths love to put restrictions on you. What not to eat, when to eat, how much of a gap between taking medicine and drinking water, etc. Plus, an impossible regime of drugs. I mean, dissolve two pills in water, give a clockwise rotation with a spoon, take a spoonful, retain the rest, give 10 jerks next time, etc. It is difficult to remember and follow, especially if you are working.

6) They often do not reveal their medicine names. If you go to another doctor, you have no record of past treatment - what worked and what did not. Coupled with point 3 above, you can't be sure if you were and are on the proper regimen.

7) Finally, anyone can claim to be a homoeopath. You don't need a formal qualification. You need a couple of books (like Darbari, Materia Medica, etc.), a chest of magic potions, immense self-confidence and patience with your patients.

II

But I would like to write in defence of Homeopathy too.

You might have discovered some research article that says Homeopathy is just another placebo. It is ineffective.

Such research, I suspect sponsored by large drug companies, regularly appears to show alternate ways of medication in a poor light - Homeopathy, Unani, Ayurveda, Chinese, etc.

Modern medication (called allopathy or English medicine in India) has made rapid strides, especially in critical care, surgical procedures, and dreaded diseases (primarily civilisation and lifestyle-related). Modern medicines are research-based, down to understanding the workings of human biochemistry at the cellular levels and keen recording of evidence of the interplay of chemical medicine and its effect on the human body and diseases.

It also attracts billions of dollars of investment and is guided solely on return on investment. For example, cancer attracts more dollar investment than Ebola simply because the latter affects people with low incomes in remote Africa.

It is debatable if modern medicines improve the quality of life (and average lifespan), and I doubt if enough research is carried out to find out why diseases like cancer are on the rise. As a statistical measurement, only 2 % of diseases are cured. The rest are managed, or their effects are lessened and rendered bearable.

So, what is the problem with traditional medicines, including Homeopathy?

First, it does not attract the brightest, which has a cascading effect on teaching, research, and student motivation. Not enough money goes into research, either.

By its very nature, Homeopathy has a many-to-many relationship between medicine and diseases (unlike many-to-one, with clear cause-effect evidence for modern medication). The timing and sequencing of medicines, potency, and the interplay of the individual constitution and behaviour of the patient further complicate it.

This means a homoeopath should be very bright, well-read, a great observer, well-researched, and trust (and document) his knowledge. Homeopathy is as much an art as a pure science.

We get doctors who are neither well-trained nor have adequate measurement support. In short, lots of self-taught quacks. And when you do not have evidence, you talk through it, right? So, they become egotistic, boastful doctors who lack self-confidence.

The problem is not with Homeopathy but with the practitioners and funding for research.

I have seen enough cases of homoeopathic miracles, but to respect patients' dignity, I would not like to dwell upon them. Suffice it to say that lots of people are walking today, thanks to

Homeopathy.

All fields of medication should work in conjunction to improve the quality of life. And not look at other sciences pejoratively.

POLITICS & GOVERNANCE

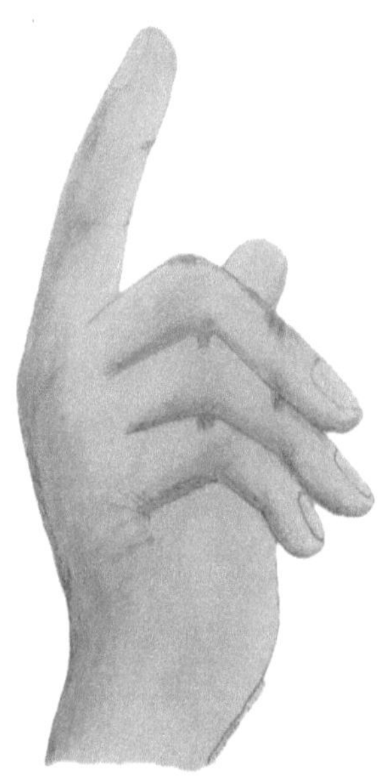

24
Let Us Talk Politics

Benefits should be conferred gradually; and in that way they will taste better.
- Niccolo Machiavelli

Let me talk politics - with socio-political overtones, without any passion and acrimony.

Admittedly, Congress played a pivotal role in the Indian independence struggle, had tall leaders (as most mass movements, especially independence movements, generated), and reaped rich dividends after the independence. They could rule India uninterrupted for 30 long years—the longest for any political dispensation that led an independence movement anywhere in the world. Next was the ANC (African National Congress, South Africa), which could get 16 years of uninterrupted rule at the end of apartheid.

It is not that Congress was homogeneous or that Indian masses were one. Far from it. We have always been a fractured State, with a few common themes binding us together - pilgrimage, sacred texts, religion, pantheon's, practices, and our unique *Varnashrama* (yes, it divided but also united when you consider the geographic expanse. (Note - *Varnashrama* is the ancient Hindu stages of life consisting of the student, the householder, the anchorite and the religious mendicant). Also on temporal dimension it connects with hoary past or cruel discrimination, depending on your position in the varnashrama). But, the sagacity of the founding fathers and the nascent nation-state's collective consciousness and euphoria (and anxiety) ensured that it remained drowned under a common purpose. The undercurrent remained. What my Professor called 'a thousand cuts, crisscrossing the nation.' We are stratified, and an Indian has multiple identities and allegiances. We can fall into scores of buckets and share one with someone who is in a different bucket in some other strata.

Congress was the holy Ganga for multiple interest groups. But it also brilliantly ensured that stratification remained in people's consciousness. Castes, Dalits, Reservations, Mandalization, Minority, Interest groups, classes, etc., ensured that people's identities stayed active and could be mass-engineered and manipulated.

It was true, especially for the Hindus.

Do recall that at election times, political dispensations appeal to various Hindu castes, but the Muslims are bracketed as one. No one appeals separately to Shia, Sunnis, Ahmadis, etc.

Congress also ensured poverty, high dependence on government doles, and low levels of education. It also started the practice of vote buying, putting dummy candidates and spreading mass disinformation.

What has changed in the last two decades or more?

1) Regional satraps have appropriated caste games, social stratification and appeal to narrow but dominant groups. It undercuts Congress' hold on these vote banks.

2) The rise of the Internet has ensured the democratisation of information and directly taken messages to the voters (avoiding traditional intermediaries like newspapers, which were managed earlier by power groups and business interests). The BJP is playing this game very well now.

3) People's rising aspirations are partly due to gradual prosperity and partly due to information access.

The time was ripe to appeal to people's higher consciousness, to rise above narrow allegiance to a more significant allegiance (Hindu and not Yadav). To see bigger dreams, to aspire for more, and to be better than others. To grow...

The crass support by so-called liberals to the blatantly anti-national stance of several groups and micro-movements and its coloured dissemination strengthened anti-congress sentiments.

I think Congress has not yet understood the paradigm shift, and regional satraps have yet to fathom that India has changed fundamentally.

Shining India was premature. Rising India is just in time.

It is not the EVM (E;ectronic Voting Machine) which is at fault. It is the change in society that some had the perspicacity to understand, while others were smug in their past glory.

25

Alternative Narrative

Life is like a game of cards. The hand that is dealt you is determinism; the way you play it is free will.
- Jawaharlal Nehru

I voted for the BJP during the last general elections. I was sick of corruption, crony capitalism, unequal development, sickening genuflection before the first family, dynastic politics, and crass opportunism. I may vote for the BJP during the next election, as I am impressed with Modiji's dynamism, hard work, and farsightedness.

But, I am very Nehruvian in my idea of India - Plural, inclusive, casteless and creedless, secular and striving to bring the fruits of progress and dignity to the last person. India is a collective consciousness and shall remain home to all those who believe in the idea of India.

Yet, I am not oblivious to the various forces tearing us apart. Those who advocate vivisection of the nation, those who dream of setting up a Caliphate in India or bringing the glory of the Vatican to India—they cannot be my friends, only fellow countrymen. I shall fight them at the level of ideas, not through violence. I shall understand them and try to address their concerns and reason with them.

The same goes for the extreme views I keep receiving in various WhatsApp groups and other social media, as happened yesterday. It reminds me of insinuation in Nazi Germany that brought untold misery and, ultimately, a fratricidal war on humanity.

It causes extreme discomfiture to me and, I am sure, massive insecurities among my fellow citizens who do not share my faith.

My fellow citizens are free to practice any faith, have their belief system, and follow and advocate their political views. It cannot be otherwise. We have many examples, including in our neighbourhood, where nations have degraded into brute majoritarianism and have no space for alternate thought processes, belief systems or practices.

If I wish to see what kind of nation I want to leave behind, I will look into the eyes of the toddler clinging to her mother's breast when I go for my walk at the park. The toddler, who cannot talk, does not know her religion and caste and cannot decide for herself. I want to leave a nation behind that she can be proud of. We have not inherited a Nehruvian or Sanatan nation. We have merely borrowed it from the next generation. We are just custodians.

I am fully aware that, as a nation, we have underachieved. We have not been able to do justice to millions. We have inculcated several things that we should be ashamed of as a nation - violence, rape, acid attack, riots...But, if we are united, we can root out everything terrible eating into our society.

When white light passes through a prism, it splits into seven colours. Imagine seven colours entering an inverse prism and unifying into a white light as it emerges from the other side. My notion of nationhood is like that inverse prism.

That is the Nehruvism of a Modi supporter.

P.S. This write-up was written before the 2019 General Elections

26

Liberalism and Nation State

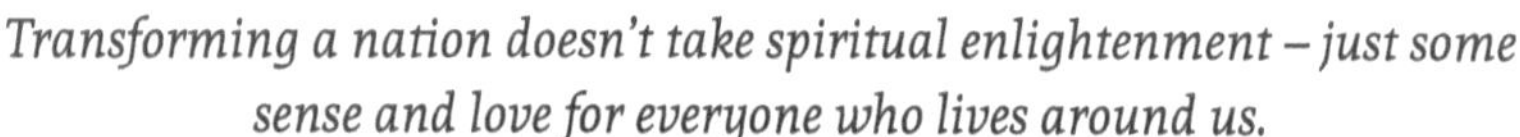

Transforming a nation doesn't take spiritual enlightenment – just some sense and love for everyone who lives around us.
- Sadhguru Vasudev Jaggi

Liberalism is a set of moral, social, and political philosophies that profess individual liberty, freedom, equality, welfarism, democracy, internationalisation, open arms embrace, etc. In short, it is a set of enlightened beliefs that most of us relate to and would genuinely believe in.

Why do liberal values, especially political ones, often conflict with the state?

Nation (the people, who identify as one) State (the geographical contours) has a strong survival instinct. This translates into securing borders and the need for strong defence at the cost of welfare measures.

It also includes putting a lid on fissiparous tendencies through policing, snooping around and control of dissent. All nation-states do it—insecure, failing nations, nations with a history of colonialism and conflicts are illiberal to a greater extent and self-assured nations to a lesser extent. I am unsure how many countries would be comfortable with the 'break the nation' slogans at a university.

States also need to assure their inhabitants of their viability and purpose. This, in turn, translates into comparison— the so-called versus debate. For example, versus debt-ridden Pakistan, versus authoritarian China, versus fundamentalist Middle East, versus decadent West, versus Poor Africa. All the current problems are laid at the door of someone else—because of Mughal, colonialism, terrorism at borders, global protectionism.

States ensure that it seeps into the minds of their people at the formative stage itself, with textbooks glorifying their past, civilisation, advancements, pantheons, scriptures, religion, philosophy, and superiority vis-a-vis other contemporary civilisations.

As we grow, the raw liberal values starkly conflict with what we have learnt. The strict rational explanation, crucible of proof and test, and constitutional resorts to press for even our just demands start militating against age-old beliefs injected into our DNA by the state throughout our lives.

This elitism is visible in most liberals. For example, their accoutrements, avocations and interests, or their assiduous attempt to look like masses (in crumpled clothes) but unwilling to engage with the common masses. Rubbing shoulders with the bigwigs and membership in elite clubs and think tanks do take liberals away from the pulse of the masses. And support for causes such as the armed struggle for equality, howsoever romantic it may seem, does attract the state's ire - remember the 'survival instinct'

Communism and its other camouflage, socialism, is not liberal by any stretch of the imagination. Communists are the worst perpetrators of violence and suppression of human dignity & liberty in their quest for equal outcomes and not equal opportunity. It suits modern-day communists to masquerade themselves as champions of liberal causes, but we all know their dark past.

Demagogues seek to exploit this schism by accentuating the fear of the unknown and insecurity and pandering to the pride, prejudices, and pantheons of their populace. No wonder liberal values, as an instrument of state governance, are in retreat.

Our founding fathers had the sagacity to understand this potential conflict between liberal and conservative values. That is why the Constitution, however pompous, progressive, and egalitarian it may appear, imposes 'reasonable restrictions' on the fundamental rights of liberty and equality.

What should the liberals do? In my view, a few simple steps

1) Stop being contemptuous of people and their deep-rooted faith. It is OK if people believe their ancestors had made great strides in medical sciences. Do not seek proof and rational explanation for every belief.

2) Leave religion alone and equality in religious affairs for a later fight. Societies change slowly, but gradualism is sustainable, secular in direction, and easy to achieve.

3) Engage with people. Hear them out, communicate, and keep an open mind. Liberty of belief is a fundamental liberal principle. It is okay to disagree rather than be disagreeable.

4) One does not need to be demonstrably liberal. You do not need to wear it up your sleeves; ready to flaunt it at all times. Do not stand out like a sore thumb.

5) Start practising what you preach. Most liberals become very illiberal when it comes to views contrary to theirs, including right-wing rants. They also have a voice, a constituency, and sometimes a genuine issue and grouse.

27
Altering History

A university stands for humanism, for tolerance, for reason, for the adventure of ideas and for the search for truth
- Jawaharlal Nehru

As school students, our parents expected us to secure the highest possible marks, which was key to obtaining admission to good institutes.

This meant writing answers that the books taught and appealed to the examiner. So, we were not to question the print. We were not mature enough to think beyond what was taught in class or written in textbooks.

While Sciences, Mathematics, and objectively verifiable subjects like Geography allowed little scope for interpretation, History, Political Sciences, and Economics allowed the authors to incorporate their perspectives (read biases).

The juvenile mind is impressionable, and the founding fathers missed no opportunity to mould the wet clay through their interpretation of these subjects, of course, through the pen of textbook writers.

So, we never questioned the text and imbibed it for two or three generations because the same party was in power for most of Independent India. The others, whenever they came to power, were for too short a duration to alter the narrative, except for minor tinkering.

And, if they attempt to change the course text now, all of us who have drank from the same fountainhead find it hard, odd and WRONG. We are 'intellectuals' who are coloured in the same dye.

Welcome to the brave new world of the Internet and social media. The 'other side' has taken to it as if there is no tomorrow. The pendulum has swung fully. Through the constant bombardment of social media messages, everything that we read is sought to be questioned.

In typical overcorrection, revivalism and ancient glory, howsoever improbable it may seem, is sought to be dished out in the name of history, medicinal sciences, surgery, economics and ancient political system of glory.

A balanced view should be illuminating.

I have compiled a few questions that challenge what I was taught in school and what I wrote on my answer sheets year after year. Some are reflective and do not admit to easy answers.

1) Was the Indian National Congress the only entity that fought for our Independence? Can the Muslim League and many other efforts, including the so-called 'militants', be rightfully scorned or talked about condescendingly in history books?

2) Were all congressional leaders secular, as we understand the term today? Would they be happy to be part of the current Congress?

3) Congress was full of prominent lawyers. How many of these took up cases for 'prisoners of conscience' facing the gallows or lengthy incarceration? Were they too expensive?

4) If Congress was a large umbrella organisation, what happened to the progeny of these freedom fighters? How come we hear of one or two families and history books talk ad nauseam about them only?

5) It is well known that the Raj favoured those supporting them with hefty land grants and other favours. These included large landholders and princely states. The same was denied to those opposing the Raj. Are not the former now much richer (given the value of their land) and much more prominent in public life, as they

had a head start in political lessons?
    Time to reflect, if not alter?

73

28

Majoritarianism

"*A nation's character is gauged by how secure and integrated the minorities feel*", so goes the popular liberal philosophy.

But how disunited the country becomes, how divisive public life becomes, and how insecure its citizens become can be gauged by how the majority starts perceiving it as discriminatory and unequal vis a vis the minorities.

I have deliberately selected the term 'Perception' - this is how people feel, not necessarily how it is.

Fanning of majority sentiments has led to disaster for nations and world peace indeed if we look at the European examples in the pre-war era. And the worst sufferers are the minorities - religious, ethnic, linguistic, social, geographic or gender.

Unfortunately, judicial activism is currently stoking the fire of majority sentiments. Demagogues and ill-intentioned divisive forces are leaving no stone unturned to add fuel to the fire and accentuate the feeling of unfairness, thereby creating enmity between the majority and the minority.

I am sharing below a few examples to put across my points.

1) *Banning of crackers during Diwali.* Just reflect on this. This is the most insignificant factor of all the causes of air pollution. Air is

polluted even before the first crackers burst. The court has not given detailed justification, not to mention any reference to scholarly unbiased research on this topic. The fact is that vehicular emissions, burning or crop remains, and deforestation cause more and long-lasting damage to the environment, which is ignored.

Couple this with the perception that only Hindu minority festivals are discriminated against—Holi for water waste and Ganapati immersion for water pollution, for instance. New Year celebrations, Bakrid, etc., are omitted.

And what is accentuating the anger? Booking of kids for bursting crackers who are found in violation of apex court orders.

2) *Entry of women at Sabarimala.* A progressive issue of gender equality could have been addressed through dialogue. Judicial activism has precipitated a religious crisis. It highlights the government's use of temple funds, control of the temple, and misuse of funds by the state. Battle lines have hardened, and liberal activists with no religious predilection have jumped into the fray.

And what is adding fuel to the fire? The scores of arrested devotees who violated apex court orders are not given bail, which a court finds 'Bad Precedence'. In contrast, the same court is not worried about providing bail to a rapist pastor, even though the prime witness dies in mysterious circumstances.

3) *Celebrations.* We have problems with renaming places, erecting statues, and building Ram temples, but in my home state, Tipu Jayanti has been celebrated for no specific reason for the last four years.

Isn't this adding fuel to the fire? Well, Tipu Suntan was a big tormentor of Hindus during his reign.

The point is not who is right or who is wrong. Both sides are dim-witted, emotional ignoramus, and it just takes a spark to kindle a conflagration.

As we witness in several states, a sense of majority isolation leads to majority consolidation. This is precisely why the grand old party is on a Temple Run. They can see the writing on the wall.

A pendulum never stands still - it always swings to the extreme. To remind one of the childhood stories, the life force of the majoritarianism demon resides in a parrot called minorities.

It is a pity that, in the process, issues of livelihood, development, empowerment, justice, and economic liberation are neglected.

29
Rewriting History

We are not makers of history. We are made by history.
- Martin Luther King, Jr.

I was at the International Book Fair at Pragati Maidan, Delhi, a few years back. I visited the Pakistan pavilion, and a book on history caught my attention. Since the book had already been sold, I could only get enough time to review the chapter headings and synopses.

But, what I found unmistakably was that the entire Pakistani history, right from its genesis, consisted of people belonging to a single faith. The author sought to link Nadir Shah's invasion to the spread of Islam, which led to the creation of the pious land. We, of course, have been taught that Nadir Shah was a plunderer. Other figures, like Tamerlane (*Taimur Lung* in Hindi), were also shown positively. Of course, the Mughal period was the pinnacle of glory in the subcontinent. The independence movement was essentially a war to establish religious identity.

There was complete silence on what I believed was an essential aspect of the cultural history of modern-day Pakistan: Taxila, Harappa, etc. These belonged to the pre-Islamic era and are at odds with the alternate narrative built through this history book.

Of course, every country has a right to seek and teach history as they see it.

My focus in this write-up is on politico-religion, which tints the cultural accomplishments of a nation-state.

I find it particularly galling that several Muslim-majority nations have sought to deny, denigrate, dissipate, disintegrate and delete the rich cultural and architectural history of their pre-Islamic period. You may look at Indonesia and Malaysia. There is a serious attempt to trace their history from the advent of Islam in their respective nations and underplay their otherwise glorious past from the earlier era. Just compare them with Buddhist neighbours such as Thailand, Cambodia, etc. (to some extent, it is true in Sri Lanka, where the cultural map underplays the artefacts and Pantheon from the Ramayana period).

If one were to look at Middle East Asia, one would observe that vast swathes of land have been deserts and could not have sustained a prosperous civilisation. Many nations have a history of Bedouin tribes, which had internecine fights and eked out living through plunders. Nations such as Jordan, Syria, Iraq, Israel and Egypt have a rich pre-Islamic civilisation. But these have been largely secular nations. Their cultural heritage (pagan or Roman-influenced) was mammoth and could not be avoided. You cannot brush pyramids under the carpet.

But, leaving these aside, there has been a sustained attempt to ignore or even destroy pre-Islamic civilisation. The destruction of the Bamiyan Buddhas in Afghanistan, the looting of the Mesopotamia Museum in Iraq, and the recent destruction of scores of pre-historic artefacts in Syria are just examples.

More subtly, Pakistan has sought to tear itself away from its glorious past.

India did suffer a prolonged Christian occupation, but she did not witness the widespread destruction of her cultural heritage. Many of it was discovered and nurtured by right-minded Christian missionaries. Possibly, our heritage was monumental. Limited proselytisation was achieved by conquering mind and body, not destroying spirit and history.

I reflect that, unlike polytheistic religions like Hinduism, Monotheistic and congregational religions, especially Islam, have not been comfortable with living with their current religious identity.

God does not like competition, I guess.

30
Politics Along Fault Lines

I will not let anyone walk through my mind with their dirty feet
- Mahatma Gandhi

Displaying great foresight and sagacity, our founding fathers very consciously selected a democratic political order that provided for universal adult suffrage but no proportional representation. It also did not provide a separate electorate along national fault lines like religion or caste.

However, they did provide educational and religious freedom to the minorities so that they could preserve their unique identity and beliefs and not be swept away under the tyranny of majoritarianism.

The underlying philosophy for an ancient civilisation but nascent nation-state was that the nation belongs to everyone, and we are collectively responsible for the welfare and wellbeing of each other. If an Akhlaq was lynched (A mob lynched him to death for allegedly carrying beef in India), it should pain Hindu brethren enough to question, seek justice and, indeed, punish the political dispensation.

Over the years, distortions crept in, and we started discussing interest groups, voting blocks, or even 'vote banks'. These assets could be used to win elections, flex muscles, and even be the subject of negotiations and vote transfers. In some way, the electorates were monetised and rendered as transferable assets.

If one looks carefully, no granularity of voting pattern is available below booth level. And booths are mixed (until recently, votes across booths were mixed, too, during counting). So, how do we procure data related to caste and religion-based voting patterns?

The answer is that these are not based on actual voting but on sample surveys by private parties. All statistical inferences suffer from biases, uncertainties, and probabilistic callisthenics.

Is it fair to make a deterministic inference about voting patterns based on sample surveys and analysis using translucent data processing tools?

Analysis of voting patterns based on caste and religion is terrible, even for the communities concerned. Those who get the lion's share, election after election, take the voting group for granted. And for those who do not vote, the elected members take no steps to meet even the genuine grievances of the community concerned.

Yet, TV debates, newspapers, and social media are full of election analyses based on these fault lines. Even after, it has been proved that voters make rational decisions and rise above narrow and parochial confines.

For far too long, fear has been used to affect the voting patterns of minority or vulnerable groups. Continuation of election analysis on this basis must add to the uncertainty.

While it is understandable that politicians shall fish in the troubled water and create and accentuate fault lines to 'divide and rule', the same by social commentators, academicians, and journalists intrigues me.

A generation or two of intellectuals in this country have made their careers analysing caste—and religion-based politics. It is difficult for them to grow out of it.

The good thing is that the younger generation, at least in cities, has stopped being caste-centric. My next generation does not know (or care for) its caste or Gotra. And what is proper for cities today shall be valid for semi-urban areas and villages in a decade or two.

One hopes that when this generation grows, it will analyse a polity based on universal and egalitarian values and essential dimensions of national life, including equality, economic growth, justice, freedom, opportunities, security, public services, international stature, peace, and happiness.

Then, only Ambedkar's vision of a casteless society will find an expression.

Fault lines are not necessarily bad. A multicultural and diverse society with a mosaic of world views is infinitely preferable to a stifling unitary view.

Anyone who bakes homemade biscuits would tell you that you must draw fault lines on the rolled-out dough before baking. This makes the biscuits crunchy.

31
School Prayer

The intellectual debt of Europe to Sanskrit literature has thus been undeniably great; it may perhaps become greater still in the years that are to come.
- Arthur A. MacDonell

I stood at the centre of the sparsely decorated room; eyes clenched, palms tightly joined together, reciting it for the millionth time.

Our Father who art in heaven,
Hallowed be thy name.
Thy kingdom come.
Thy will be done
on earth as it is in heaven.
Give us this day our daily bread,
and forgive us our trespasses,
as we forgive those who trespass against us,
and lead us not into temptation,
but deliver us from evil.

I was being prepared for a school admission interview, which was expected to be my X factor for getting into the only English-medium convent school in the town. Since I was not precisely precocious, I needed to practice it repeatedly.

Having secured my admission, I would have recited it hundreds of times during the morning prayer congregation. I never asked what it meant, who wrote it, or why I was reciting it. It was part of the daily rigmarole. Period.

And I remained a Hindu throughout, even though I recited a Catholic prayer from the New Testament all those years.

Much later, several members of my generation and the next generation studied at missionary schools and must have recited this or similar prayers thousands of times. Their faith remained unaltered. If they took any lesson, it was that they would not send their children to missionary school, as they felt these schools sacrificed education at the altar of discipline.

So, how come this wonderful verse from *Upanishad* has become so controversial?

Asato mā sadgamaya
tamasomā jyotir gamaya
mrityormāamritam gamaya
Oṁ śhānti śhānti śhāntiḥ

[From ignorance, lead me to truth;
From darkness, lead me to light;
From death, lead me to immortality
Om peace, peace, peace]

A petition, currently being heard at the Apex court, claims that this prayer recited daily at Central government schools, influences young minds and is not in keeping with our secular traditions. For records, the prayer has been recited for ages.

The verse is called *Shanti Mantra* (prayer of peace) from the *Brihadaranyaka Upanishad*, one of the 108 *Upanishads*. It deals with life in exile (forest). *Upanishads*, by the way, literally mean 'Sitting down near.' These Vedanta teachings were imparted by the teachers at the Gurukuls.

As you can see, the meaning is quite ennobling - a prayer to lead one to truth, to light and to immortality.

If the objection is that it is in Sanskrit, mottos in Sanskrit are pretty standard, from the Apex Court to the armed forces to educational institutions. One of the most appropriate ones is LIC's *Yogakshemam Vahamyaham* (I arrange for securing what they lack and preserving what they have), which is from *Bhagavad Gita*.

Is the court planning to do away with all these?

I hope the Apex Court does not believe that the morning congregation and prayer are antithetical to the current ethos. Children need some common bonding in this era of individualism.

The only objection is that this prayer is from a Hindu scripture. My rude response is that we had to go back a thousand years or more to seek an ennobling message, as the current secular generation was incapable of writing something substantial that was equally deep but cogent.

In middle school, we had an essay titled '*Asto Ma Sadgamaya*' in chaste Hindi. Vinoba Bhave authored this essay. Bhave Ji was a saintly Gandhian who signified self-abnegation and Spartan living. For records, Vinoba Bhave was a Jain mendicant.

It would appear to a casual bystander that the Apex Court is rummaging at the bottom of the barrel to take out cases to hear and keep judges busy. By the way, it is estimated that over two lakh cases are pending at the Supreme Court itself.

I just wanted to let you know that I rest my case.

Asto Ma Sadgamaya

32
The Way Government Works!

———❧———

Just as it is impossible to know when a swimming fish is drinking water, so it is impossible to find out when a government servant is stealing money
- Chanakya

You are justifiably inconvenienced at having to disclose your Aadhar number in addition to your PAN (Permanent Account is the tax identifier number in India) number. Why two numbers?

But spare a thought for the corporates. A compendium of various numbers and forms is as follows. I am sure this is not an all-inclusive list.

First, you need a company registration number (CIN), which the Registrar of Companies allocates.

Then, Income Tax allocates PAN and TAN (Tax Deduction and Collection). I never understood why these numbers should be different. But then, the central tax authority follows its own logic. To confound you further, a financial year is not enough, so they created an assessment year.

Just hold on. You forgot TIN (Taxpayer Identification) or VAT (Value Added Tax, since replaced by GST - Goods and Service Tax) —one for each state. Its purpose is unknown, except if you order some goods, the supplier needs this lest an inspector stop the delivery vehicle.

Then you have a Service tax number (merged into GST now), one for each activity you undertake, potentially five or more. Now, it has been replaced by GST. One needs several of these.

No, I did not forget Professional Tax. You have two for each state—one for the company and the other for submitting employees' contributions. If you are an all-India company, there are around 50 such numbers.

Then, there is the Provident Fund—one for the company and two for each employee—one is a permanent number called UAN (Universal Account), and the other is employer-specific.

Are you already bored? But I am not finished yet. The IEC code for importers and exporters, the ESIC code for employee insurance (and the subcode for each state), and the subcode for each state are other identifiers that corporations need.

Then, states have their pound of flesh. Each state needs shop and establishment registration for each office unit, and one needs to file returns for each. Each is equally cumbersome and adds no value to the corporation or the state.

There are a few more. For example, employment exchange returns, POSH (Prevention of Sexual Harassment) returns, form D for bonus disclosure, form A for gratuity, workers compensation returns, Labor welfare fund returns, contract Labor returns under form U, minimum wages return, and a series of returns under form R 24*7, form P, form Q, form D, form B, form A and am omnibus form T.

Now, mind you, all the above are state-specific. So, you have variations for each state and must file as many times as necessary, some online and some on paper.

If you still have time after all the compliances, you can do what you have set up your establishment for—manufacture, sell, pay a salary, and make some profit.

If you think you are being compliant by doing all these things, think again. The state has ways to find noncompliance. Indeed, they can find a clause under which you are non-compliant.

If you are non-compliant, you will receive a notice, and the helpful Inspector will tell you to work with a consultant who will ensure your compliance. Please do not ask me about the consultant's background.

33

Red Beckon

A people that values its privileges above its principles soon loses both.
- Dwight D. Eisenhower

The banning of red beckon on politicians' and bureaucrats' vehicles has been widely welcomed, even if political dispensation has rushed to take credit for it. It was a nuisance and an antithesis to our democratic and egalitarian values. At the same time, demands have been raised to do more. *Ye dil mange more* (This heart asks for more).

Let us examine these.

Politicians and officials holding high positions are exposed to physical harm, and they need protection. It is provided all over the world. So long as these are not obtrusive and are reviewed periodically, I see no harm in retaining them.

However, what is galling is that these genuine needs of a few have been misused by all and sundry, such as not standing in queues at airports (which are pretty secure), not stopping at traffic lights, making even ambulances give way to their cavalcade, large entourage, gun-wielding police officers, and general throwing around weight. It is time for a code of conduct to be set up and those violating these to be taken to severe task by parliament, the executive branch, or the judiciary.

Similarly, some benefits, such as housing, telephone calls, and petrol charge reimbursement, are justified, as our representatives need to meet their constituents. But why do we need a business class seat (and ego) for our legislators? This needs to be done away with. Let them travel like us.

There is a case to review housing entitlement in Lutyens' Delhi. Most Bungalows are from the British period and are crumbling. Through imaginative planning, there is a need to rebuild, modernise, and create more capacity. Given the price of land, it can be done with nearly no additional burden on taxpayers. The minister's suggestion to move junior ministers to apartments is welcome. The same applies to states and districts, too.

The third category includes salary and other non-cash benefits such as paid staff, subsidised food, etc. Indeed, there is a strong case for converting all these to salary benefits and taxing them, just like you and me.

One India, one law.

Happily, steps have been taken in this direction, such as eliminating subsidised food at parliament.

Much has been made about the salaries of legislators and ministers. This is a perception issue, as they get to revise their own salaries. If compared with their salaries in the fifties, I do not think their current pay is disproportionate.

What is needed is a salary and benefits commission, which should fix their base salary.

Legislators' salaries should be linked to GDP growth. A variable 'bonus' component should be based on achieving annual goals or 'key performance measures' at the constituency level. These could be objective, national-level bipartisan goals such as setting up schools, enrolment and retention, mid-day meal coverage, meeting literacy goals, abolition of begging and child labour, setting up hospitals, reducing crime and road accidents, etc.

Following a parliamentary debate, I recall that a word starting with 'P' referring to untouchability was banned. The time has come to banish another term from our Lexicon. It is a three-letter acronym starting with 'V', and I can assure you, it is not 'vicissitude'

34
Educating The Masses

If you want to destroy the civilisation of a nation, there are three ways
1. Destroy family structure. 2. Destroy education. 3. Lower their role
models

- Anonymous

Did you know that until the mid-seventies, China's GDP was the same as India's? Now, it is three times as much.

While we can debate endlessly, until cows return home, why China grew much faster, one inescapable fact remains: China invested massively in education. At the same time, we paid, in considerable measure, lip service.

Even today, when I see children playing on the streets or begging at traffic junctions at hours when they should be at school, I feel sad that we are continuing to add illiterates to society.

Yet, it is not beyond us to reverse the situation and reap rich dividends. We have the demographic advantage.

Education primarily consists of five elements.

1) *Infrastructure* - Schools, classrooms, library, books, computer centre, living facility for teachers and student meals. It includes bussing students to the nearest school. My calculation shows that this is something achievable at our current GDP over a period of 5 to 10 years

2) *Pedagogy* - Designing the curriculum, teaching methods and assessment in tune with needs - not today's needs, but two decades

from now. Technology can provide an enormous base for improving teaching methods. And we have enough knowledgeable and well-intentioned people to improve the present pedagogy.

3) *Enrolment* - Creating awareness of how education helps one gain employment and improve one's standard of living and quality of life is essential to ensuring high enrolment and retention.

4) *Pricing* - While elementary education should be free, secondary education should be heavily subsidised, but there is little reason to subsidise higher education. Instead, it should move to a loan model. Higher education centres may also fund themselves through commercially usable research and IPR generation, seeking endowments, alum networks, placement fees and such innovative means. It also underscores the need for the government to provide education through funded schools of the same quality as the private schools offered at usurious fees.

5) *Quality of teachers* - Admittedly, this is the biggest challenge. Creating well-equipped and motivated teachers is not easy, and there are no easy answers.

If one looks at other nations, one would observe that teachers are respected, well paid, well looked after, and provided with job security. Teachers' pensions in the USA are one example. As the result shows, it is the opposite in India.

I offer my suggestions for improving teaching standards.

1) Incentivize teachers to gain skills, such as passing challenge exams, including in IT usage. Link disproportionate increments to acquiring new skills.

2) Ensure teachers get paid on time. With universal banking and mass salary processing, this is immensely possible

3) Measure outcome, not expenditure. Incentivise teachers for attaining specific goals, such as 100% literacy in particular areas or all adults passing board-level examinations.

4) Make teachers part of the local community. Let them have a stake in creating awareness and coming close to the community they serve. Let them innovate teaching methods to suit local needs and incentivise them to grow beyond the narrow boundary of the

four walls of the school. For example, adult literacy when schools are not used (usually evening), disseminating agriculture-related awareness, etc.

II

My domestic help came to me seeking financial support for her children's school education. The fees, at Rs 90,000 per annum for two kids, were well over three months of her income. The entire fees for the year were to be paid in advance and were nonrefundable.

Her children go to a local private English school named after Mother Teresa. It has classes up to 10th standard and an arrangement to appear for school finals through another school. The school was recommended by someone equally ill-qualified to judge the quality of education. Parents did not know about the curriculum, exam pattern, affiliation, etc. They only hoped that once their children were educated, they would enjoy a better life than their parents. You would readily agree that their sacrifice for investing in their children's future was far greater than yours and mine. And their hopes were more modest yet brittle.

On enquiry, she said that the local government schools are free, but teachers hardly come; they make children run errands and do not bother whether children come to class. In short, teaching was far away from their minds. They are Government servants with similar hubris and lack of sense of responsibility or accountability. Anyway, the choice of school is a parental prerogative.

If you ask me, this is a much bigger scam and a micro-level crony capitalism. We recruit teachers not to teach but to create employment, especially for those who are otherwise unemployable but are either well-connected or willing to grease palms. A friend who works with teachers of unaided schools in North Karnataka to augment their income and improve their teaching skills informs me that nearly three-fourths of them are unteachable.

Unlike China, which made massive investments in basic education through the 1970s—all teaching in their mother tongue—and is reaping the benefits today, we have created an inefficient and corrupt educational bureaucracy and an educational mafia.

How would you explain an English private school fleecing parents in the name of education? How would you explain barely educated, ill-paid teachers teaching children through rote and giving them liberal marks in internal examinations to keep parents' hopes alive? I know it with certainty, as my mother was helping these kids recently and realised that the one attending 6th standard could not write error-free simple sentences or read or recite if the content was not from a textbook (which he had memorised). Please make no mistake, they were pretty bright kids and, with some support, picked up at astonishing alacrity and perspicacity.

I did not have the heart to ask her what this education would fetch her children. We bemoan a lack of development, opportunities, and reservations. We worry about cows, talaq, and moral vigilantes.

To conclude, my mind goes back a few decades to when I worked on an educational project with a local NGO. They were running a school for underprivileged children from slums and faced dropouts and chronic absenteeism. I met the parents, and they asked me, "*If we send our children to school, bear it out for 11 years or so, will our children get jobs like you?*" He was asking if teaching also develops fungible and monetisable skills.

I had no answer then. Unfortunately, I don't have an answer now, either. In two decades, nothing has changed. Possibly, too short a time in the nation's history. However, it took too long for a new generation of illiterate people to fill the job market. Where jobs are scarce, a tectonic shift in employment is underway, and fissiparous forces are ready to lure them away to a vitriolic future, undermining and tearing apart the very fabric of harmonious and equitable living.

III

This lovely government school teacher couple, on a visit to Bangalore, first extended their holidays, then benefited from the government declaring holidays due to extreme winter (5 degrees Celsius), upcoming festivals, and a few French leave (wink! wink! -

this is the Indian version of the Houdini act from work). They have been employed in a relatively prosperous district in a poor part of eastern India and must commute daily to school.

"How do students manage in their absence? How about their learning?"

My question surprised them - and offended them, too.

They responded that the Government itself does not take education seriously. From elections to censuses to all sundry jobs, teachers provide the legwork for the tiring, mundane, and tedious. Why should teachers take their jobs seriously?

No wonder the latest economic survey discovered and bemoaned that only 25 per cent of students have learnt what is expected of them at their respective ages. This is pathetic compared to 90% in China and 30% in Indonesia.

Think again. Most urban and private schools do a reasonable job. This means the effectiveness of rural and government-provided education is near zero. As I type and you read, we are creating millions of uneducated and unemployable people. And millions do not even enrol or drop out early.

Make no mistake. Governments have invested heavily in educational infrastructure over the years. Even educationist Yogendra Yadav underscored that we have made sufficient progress in providing concrete and blackboard infrastructure. It is high time we looked at the quality of teachers and teaching.

Erecting physical infrastructure is easy. It requires budgetary outlay and contracting (and hence provides rent-seeking opportunity). It can be done at many locations simultaneously. Most importantly, it earns a physical "wow" demonstration of progress and intent, which can be converted into votes at husting.

What do you think about the insides of these walls? The teachers? Pedagogy? Course content? Books, computers? Evaluation? Pupil support for special needs students? Overall discipline and educational rigour?

Ironically, using technological strides, it should have been easier to take quality education to the remotest areas and multiply it rapidly. Good teachers could create world-class e-content and render insightful illustrations. Technology's ability to repeat content as often as needed could help us reach as never before. And it could transcend the physical and budgetary constraints.

Tragically, the appointment of teachers has been seen as providing jobs. Teachers are often demotivated and absent; they know very little, and at times, shamefully, they are seen taking rest in class or sending pupils to run errands.

Are we preparing our kids to face the challenges of the future? In a ruthlessly competitive and globalised world village where computers, artificial intelligence, and NLP (neuro-linguistic programming) rule and human beings' roles become increasingly constricted, what will these kids do when they grow up without quality and future-oriented educational crutches?

Even if I may seem old and grumpy, I find the curriculum severely diluted today compared to when we studied. There is too much distraction (social media, computer games), too little importance given to critical aspects of learning (Grammar, literature, history, and even science), and parents running scared of children (stress, suicide) or busy furthering their careers.

Indeed, I would not like to sit in a time machine, return to being a teenager, and live again.

Nelson Mandela is credited with saying that if you wish to destroy a nation, you must degrade its education.

Without character, formal learning, the ability to analyse and discriminate, and wisdom (*vivek*), the citizens would kill the nation.

We are doing a great job in this respect. Look around you at how reactive we have become. Sitting on a powder keg. Ready to unleash. Blinded, angry, restless...

P.S. Even today, at times, I get nightmares of exams, the rigour to which we were subjected, and some of our teachers. They were great people - a picture of self-abnegation, who sacrificed their youth to give us our future. Happily, some are connected with me and continue to bless us.

May your tribe grow.

IV

A small piece of news caught my attention amid Teacher's Day greetings and warm wishes. India has some nine million school teachers. If you add teachers at institutions of higher learning (and I am doing some guesstimates), we have around 15 million Indians in the noble profession of disseminating knowledge and skills. That is an astonishing 1.5% of our population.

We have not done enough for our teachers.

So, here is my seven-pointer wish list for our teachers that society (of which the Government is a part) should provide for

1) Clear their salary dues immediately and ensure they get them on time. If this needs centralised banking processing, so be it.

2) Work to enhance their skill sets (and weed out those who are unlearnable) in their current teaching area and the teaching needed for the future. Harness technology if it helps accelerate their learning. Incentivise teachers to acquire new skill sets with generous emoluments.

3) Immediately plan for a Teachers' Pension scheme in line with what they do in the USA. Ensure that after retirement, the teacher has a roof over one's head and an assured pension to run their household

4) Improve the working conditions of teachers and provide better tools. This includes equipped classrooms, computers, a library, hygiene and other facilities for teachers and students

5) Provide teachers with housing while on the job. Especially if they are working in far-flung areas

6) Reduce the classroom hours and allow teachers time to invest in preparing for teaching. Rather than a fixed, inflexible curriculum, let teachers customise pedagogy. If this means allowing multiple curricula, so be it.

7) Finally, give teachers the respect they deserve in society. These jobs may not pay well, but we can compensate for this by giving them the respect they deserve for building the future of our children.

If we cannot do these, exchanging greetings on Teachers' Day looks shallow, ritualistic, insincere, and dishonest.

Trust me, a $3 trillion economy can do this. We have the wherewithal to accomplish it in a decade or less. We need determination and far-sightedness.

35

Mid-Day Meals

All children should have the basic nutrition they need to learn and grow and to pursue their dreams, because, in the end, nothing is more important than the health and well-being of our children.
- Michelle Obama

Yet again, some children fall sick after consuming the mid-day meal. This happens with alarming regularity. Necessary care is possibly not taken while cooking food for children, or it is not handled by professionals. Low budgets and corruption could be contributory causes.

When we think about it, the mid-day meal was a revolutionary step in attracting and retaining children from poor, mainly rural families, to school and ensuring that they got at least one nutritious meal.

But, right from the beginning, it was beset with controversies.

Teachers were asked to double up as cooks in several schools, and their entire attention shifted to cooking rather than teaching. Then, children were asked to bring their plates, asked to clean, and sat in dingy, unhygienic corners to eat. Then, there was news of substandard food, adulteration, pilfering, etc.

I am told that in many states, parents have been involved in preparing mid-day meals, which yielded positive results.

The solution is allocating adequate funds (not half-hearted measures such as Rs 2.50 per child per day) and setting up large base kitchens.

I recall ISKCON offering to set up large base kitchens and transfer knowledge for mass-scale cooking. Mass-scale cooking is very different from wedding cooking. It needs different equipment, cooking styles, pressurised hot water, steam, special drains, and cleaning automation. Plus, it requires close quality control, including testing. In the context of children, special attention is needed to meet their nutritional needs in their growing-up phase, which requires adherence to dietary standards.

Transporting cooked and packed food from these base kitchens to schools should be possible. We do it for railways, and Mumbai Dabbawalas have won international laurels.

Why can we not adopt it for our schools?

Only a healthy nation can grow and meet future challenges. Malnourishment during childhood leads to stunted growth and lifelong debilitation.

Indeed, a three trillion economy can care for its poor children's educational and nutritional needs.

36

School Score and Success in Life

Education is what remains after one has forgotten what one has learned in school.

- Albert Einstein

I read an interesting study by a university research scholar about the correlation between academic and scholastic scores and later achievements in corporate life.

This research in the USA discovered that those scoring high (average 3.6 GPA) went ahead with their higher education, bagged decent jobs and promising careers in the corporate world.

Interestingly, those who excelled in their respective fields - so-called outstanding and outliers - had much lower scores (an average of 2.9 GPA).

Why should it be so? Do high marks guarantee success in corporate life, or is success like a roll of dice?

It is undisputed that high scores have a direct (even if not definite) correlation to scholastic learning. However, academic excellence reflects high discipline in education, curriculum conformance, and adherence to pedagogy. It also reflects well-rounded learning, ranging from mathematics to history.

This discipline and focus help secure a decent career and progress in corporate life.

However, jobs do not demand well-rounded learning - they reward excellence in specific work areas.

On the other hand, those who have a single-minded obsession are hardly conformists and, hence, do not achieve academic excellence. However, they are far more successful if their career choice matches their interests. Some of the greats, therefore, were average or even poor students. Their brilliance lay elsewhere, and they bloomed at the right time and place.

One valid criticism of our pedagogy is that it has not evolved much over decades, at least in the developing world and school learning context. It also emphasises uniform learning (one size fits all) instead of encouraging experiments, learning from failures, and recognising individual brilliance in specific, even niche areas. It also equates academic success with high scores and treats scores as an alias for students' success and the validation of their pedagogy and rigour. It discourages any avocations that do not directly lead to scores.

For success in life - success in a broader context - clarity of ideas, an uncluttered mind, structured thinking, and unravelling solutions must be encouraged. Cogent and clear communication, listening and synthesising various ideas, and developing implementable solutions must also be encouraged.

Our education system does not seem to recognise it.

37

Unreserve

---❦---

I do not like reservation in any form. Especially reservation in jobs. I am against any such step that promotes inefficiency and takes us toward mediocrity.
- Jawaharlal Nehru

So, the genie is out of the bottle. Ten per cent reservation in education and government jobs for economically backward groups (so-called general category) is sure to become a reality - political compulsions demand so. It does not matter that it would be challenged in the apex court. It also does not merit attention to where the government and public sector jobs are. And how would you identify the genuine poor?

Already, there are demands for higher reservation percentages, reservations on religious grounds, and reservations in the private sector—conscious that, in the future, more and more jobs will be created in the private sector.

I co-founded a company over a decade ago, and I do not know my colleagues' caste. It did not matter. They join us, learn, contribute, move to greener pastures, or stay with us to build a bright future for themselves. Caste lines are blurring, going by the growing trend of marriage based on one's own choice. I am happy about it.

But is it a pure meritocracy? Far from it. We consciously factor in the background - educational opportunities, family status, gender, regional disparities, opportunities, etc.- during every stage of the selection process. Not all are equally fluent in English, for example.

We discharge our social responsibility consciously and proudly by providing opportunities to work and grow, factoring in past disadvantages one might have faced. And we do not let candidates know that we are 'ignoring' some of the standard selection factors in genuine cases.

Why am I writing all these?

If a small firm like ours is so conscious about providing equity, why can't large enterprises do so? And why should the government not adopt a factor-based approach to iron out differences in background and *'handicaps'*?

Why can we not adopt point-based or factor-based ratings while providing jobs, considering gender, geography, socio-economic status, physical handicaps, etc.?

After all, wards of an IAS officer from a backward caste have different handicaps as against a rich person living in a backward region in India. Poor people from higher social strata face different challenges than rich people from a scheduled tribe.

My suggestion...Consider doing away with all reservations. Bring in a factor-based approach, based on scientific analysis of the family, with appropriate weights.

Developing a universally acceptable set of factors should be possible in a country like ours, with rich data and being at the forefront of information technology. And we have enough right-minded people to be fair in their analysis.

We can not afford another stratification of society. Provide equal opportunity. Be fair.

38

PIL on Caste

Caste is not a physical object like a wall of bricks or a line of barbed wire which prevents the Hindus from co-mingling and which has, therefore, to be pulled down. Caste is a notion; it is a state of the mind.
- B. R. Ambedkar

To,
The Honorable Chief Justice
Supreme Court of India
Mandi House, Tilak Mark
New Delhi – 110201

Your Honor,

I am pleading to draw your kind attention to the flagrant and sickening disclosure, amplification, and attribution of decisions and motives based on one's caste, creed, sect, denomination, and religious belief in a large section of mainstream media in India.

My caste is my private identity, and I have complete freedom to accept the very notion of caste & creed or to reject it altogether. It is, in my humble view, part of the right to privacy, as per the recent Supreme Court's interpretation of Article 21 relating to the right to life and personal liberty, under the chapter 'Fundamental Rights' of the Indian constitution and is guaranteed to me, as a citizen. No institution or person has any right to disclose my caste without my express permission, least of all the mainstream media and sections of the political class, who would look at every action through the prism of one's caste affiliation.

That I am a Dalit, or a high caste Hindu, Yadav or Kurmi caste, or belong to Vokkaliga or Lingayat sect, Dravidian or Aryan by belief, Shia or Sunni Muslim, Protestant or Catholic Christian, Jat or non-Jat Sikh, follow Mahayana or Hinayana Buddhism, believe in Digambar or Shwetambar Jainism should not matter to state or any other entity in this great nation. The founding fathers dreamt of a casteless society where justice is provided to all, and those suffering from socio-economic disadvantage were to be helped to overcome their handicaps, participate in nation building and reap the fruits of their labour.

Your Honor, if you agree with the above surmise, how come mainstream media houses, consisting of visual and print media, as well as their internet portals, tweet accounts and other footprints in social media, are indulging in flagrant violation of citizens' privacy to his and her identity, attribute one's success and accomplishments to one's caste affiliations, thereby not only belittling one's achievements, but also seek crooked, diabolical and Machiavellian design in every action of the state, its organ or any newsworthy action and development, even in private sphere?

A case in point is the awarding of Padma Vibhushan, India's second highest civilian award, to the great Music Maestro, Shri Ilaiyaraaja; a prominent newspaper, 'The New Indian Express,' has cast aspersions that this award was given to the maestro because of his Dalit identity and to overcome the current political dispensation losing ground to another Dalit leader in Gujarat. You can easily see that there is no connection, as Shri Ilaiyaraaja is an internationally acclaimed musician. Millions of Indians who did not know about his private identity were made aware of it.

Sometime back, when the Gujarat election results were announced and ministries formed, a portal, instead of publishing the names of ministers, gave the caste-wise breakdown of ministries.

Whenever news about a political leader is covered, their sectarian affiliation is prefixed.

Caste is a reality in India. But is it desirable to make it the pre-eminent part of one's identity and disclose it all the time, as well as analyse and attribute every action of one through the caste angle?

Your Honor, if this disease is not arrested, a day will come when the decisions of the land's highest court will also be sought to be seen through the lens of the caste of individual judges and motives attributed.

Your Honor, I beg of you that this has to end.

Some may argue that the same constitution also guarantees freedom of expression under Article 19, subject to certain limitations. I may humbly submit that your right to freedom of expression does not extend to disclosing my caste identity. Your freedom to waive your hand ceases the moment my cheek comes in the way, as they say. If this happens, then your intentions would actually need to be agitated.

In any case, it is well established that using caste slurs is unconstitutional. I may also submit that Article 15 protects one against discrimination on several grounds, including caste. Revealing my caste could undoubtedly lead to discrimination in the social milieu. I have a right to protection against any such attempt by anyone to belittle my identity and cause social discomfort.

I would, therefore, request you to treat this as a public interest litigation and issue a notice to media houses seeking them to stop disclosing - directly or indirectly - the caste, creed, sect, denomination or religious belief of individuals about whom they report. They should be proscribed from attributing motives, directly or indirectly, based on affiliation. This should apply uniformly to print media, visual media, and their electronic and social media presence through portals, tweet accounts, Facebook accounts, and other means.

If citizens attach their caste name to their first name, it is their choice. Readers can make their own interpretation if they are caste conscious. The media should not be allowed to make its readers look through the grey lens of caste all the time and accentuate it in the process.

Why only media houses? Without the oxygen of publicity, sociopolitical life will automatically readjust itself to a less fractured, less divisive, and less antiquated narrative. So long as they receive amplified publicity through the media, any thought of creating a unified Indian society is only a dream.

Your Honor, I am writing this as an Individual and am not seeking a million signatures through online campaigns. I trust in the power of one. If my cause is just, it does not matter how many signatories are at the bottom of the petition. It also does not matter that I am not a trained lawyer. In my humble view, truth must be told, and I am sure truth shall knock at the door of the highest judiciary without the need for crutches of formality and procedural rigour.

I am confident that my voice is the voice of millions of Indians who are watching the sickening degradation of media houses and their attempt to bring the caste angle to all their thinking, analysis and reporting.

I rest my case, my Lord.

39

Judiciary

Sitting on the post of a Panch, no one is anyone's friend or enemy. He can think of nothing except justice. God speaks through the tongue of the Panch.

- Munshi Premchand in Panch Parmeshwar

The beauty of sharp and bitter polarisation is that facts, fiction and innuendo, hitherto unknown, start unravelling itself. At the end of it, bitterness and bigotry remain, shorn of anything positive. All positives are permanently obliterated.

The recent fratricidal war at the Indian Supreme Court is a case in point.

I, for one, never believed that the Indian judicial system was a paragon of virtues—it was indeed not an idyllic island amid general decline and despondency.

As a college sophomore, I passionately debated the need for the judiciary to heal itself. I found Indian courts slower than sloth, blinder than Komodo monitor, and more stone-hearted than stone itself.

I would argue that the judiciary has let the victims down in mass murders, from the Nelli massacre in Assam to Bhopal to the Uphaar tragedy. The judiciary failed to protect citizens against the might of the police state and its excesses during an emergency. The judiciary could not defend itself from the shenanigans of rouge law ministers and their idiosyncrasies. That judiciary could let the rich slip through the cracks of law for financial frauds and for rash driving leading to accidents and crime, while the poor languished and vegetated in jails as an undertrial for periods far above the offence for which they were initially booked. And that the judiciary would not be sure of its wisdom, given the many contradictory judgments on critical constitutional issues and fundamental rights.

In a way, we have been naive. We trusted an institution in isolation, blinded to general decline and pervasive moral turpitude.

If you look carefully at our four estates

The legislature has long been divisive, communal, casteist and regressive.

The executive branch, so eloquently represented by its (rusted) steel-structured bureaucracy and administration, is corrupt, insensitive, and incompetent.

The less said about the self-proclaimed fourth estate - media. It is self-serving, negative (even more than this write-up!), and inflated egoists who could degrade themselves to any level.

In the scenario, the judiciary was the last vestige - a beckoning of hope.

It stands shattered now.

The internecine battle tells us that thy feet are made of wet clay within the judicial edifice.

Judges have a predilection for one political dispensation or the other. A closed collegium appoints judges - yet is not impervious to external influences. The judges fight to get high-profile cases. The cases are not mere cases - they have a hierarchy, too. The seeker of justice does not matter. The judges are juniors and seniors, and seniors look down upon the juniors' judicial abilities. The judges who quibble over 'shall', 'will' and 'may' are oblivious to their code of ethics and acceptable public behaviour.

What was keeping it all together was the power to initiate contempt.

No more so. Accusations are flying thick and fast, attracting even more libellous counteraccusations.

And my Lord, I am not telling this. Your fraternity is telling this - not in whispers, but loud.

Well, Panch Parmeswar's story was just a romantic imagination of a simpleton, rustic.

We believed we had a functioning democracy. And our institutional pillars. Right?

Well, one pillar stands erect and strong - 1.3 billion Indians, three-fourths of whom, in the brave hot summer, to the bitter bone, chilling winter, to soggy rains, stand for hours to cast their vote. And repose their trust in India.

It is their tryst with Karma.

Else, *dil ko bahlane ke liye, Galib ye khyal accha hai.* (For the sake of soothing the heart, Ghalib, this thought is good*).*

40

Fundamental Right to Privacy

Civilization is the progress toward a society of privacy. The savage's whole existence is public, ruled by the laws of his tribe. Civilization is the process of setting man free from men.

- Ayn Rand

During our growing-up years, we read about the Golaknath and the Keshvanand Bharti cases, which dealt with interpreting Fundamental rights as enshrined in the Indian constitution. Anyone caring about the disproportionate might of the State vis a vis the ordinary citizen would be well aware of the profound impact of these judgements on our fundamental rights.

Justice (Retd.) Puttaswamy vs. Union of India, otherwise known as the 'right to privacy' judgement, has now been added to this illustrious list.

In one stroke, a nine-judge bench has unanimously elevated the right to privacy to a fundamental right. I have not found a parallel where the right to privacy is a fundamental right. However, the USA and many countries protect the right to privacy as sacrosanct and is protected zealously.

While the media, in their usual flippant manner, have decided to interpret this in terms of who is the winner and who is the loser (State is the loser. One can interpret it as the ruling party, namely, the Bhartiya Janata Party, headed by PM Narendra Modi ji), the fact is that the Apex court has overturned its own judgements on this issue in the past.

That this is an ennobling moment for citizens and a sobering one for the State is obvious. But its profundity will be felt only in due course.

The most vocal voice you hear is that of the LGBTQ community. Frankly, no one cares about your sexual orientation. But why put a grotesque fluorescent mask on your eyes and parade on the street with a rainbow banner? That is beside the point for me in the context of this blog.

From sublime to the mundane. To terra firma of reality, from eloquent thoughts. How are we affected in our day-to-day life after this judgement?

Is the right to privacy analogous to the right to anonymity? Could you consider a few cases?

Can I demand that railways stop displaying reservation charts at stations and on trains containing my name, sex, and age? Instead, only show the ticket number.

Can I decline to share my personal and income information with the government? And decline information about assets, investments and overseas accounts? Will it not be unfair to honest taxpayers, bearing an ever-increasing tax burden?

Can I decline to share photocopies of various personal documents with banks, insurers, and telecom companies and still receive service?

Can I decline to share health details with insurers and, at worst, pay a higher premium?

Can I refuse to allow web companies to access and share my personal details and offer me endless products through online contextual advertisements and call centres? Can they deny me services if I disagree with their terms and conditions, which I believe infringe on my fundamental right to privacy?

And then there is the Aadhar conundrum.

The right to privacy and its limitations will be tested on the crucible of merit and interpretation in the coming months and years.

That we have fundamental rights is ennobling. Do they work on the ground, especially in villages and shanty towns? Do they stand against the might and repression of the State and its corrupt foot soldiers? And are courts, already overburdened with cases, in a position to deliver justice to us?

We have writs of Habeas corpus, Mandamus and quo warranto for records. How often are long-disappeared persons brought to court by police? How frequently can you get your work done by a recalcitrant and obnoxious State and its bureaucracy? And how does a cop or inspector react when you demand to see his delegated authority?

That, alas, is the terra firma.

41

Regulation

Under capitalism, man exploits man. Under communism, it's just the opposite.
- John Kenneth Galbraith

'*It is best to let the weak die*'.

This may appear shocking if read in the context of an individual. But, for a weak and unsustainable commercial enterprise, this is the best wish one could express.

Let us accept it. An enterprise locks in the capital, labour, and natural resources such as land and raw materials. If it cannot optimally use these resources, it is better to make way for someone better equipped to unlock and efficiently use them.

In the national economy, there is a concept of 'factor productivity'—essentially, how much bang we generate for our investments on a national aggregated scale. The more we let sick enterprise drag on, the less economic efficiency we create. This slows national growth and cascades positive externalities such as job creation, infrastructure growth, and better quality of life.

Why do enterprises fail? Internal factors such as unrealistic business plans, poor management, and bad HR practices may lead to poor employee motivation, poor quality control, and poor customer service. External factors could include technological shifts, changes in consumer taste, competition offering better solutions, cheaper imports, stifling regulations not allowing enterprises to grow, crony capitalism, and favouritism.

Unfortunately, closing an enterprise is a stigma for management, employees, and the economy. Hence, all attempts are made to keep it running—putting good money into a bad cause, so to speak. Interestingly, this is all to provide customer services and prevent monopolies from arising.

And the Government is the ultimate arbiter. Right? So, what does the Government do? **REGULATE**.

Make no mistake. It is not much different from the license quota raj when some Mandarins decided what (and how much) private enterprise should produce.

The regulator is like the school teacher, who, after giving admission, keeps a sharp eye on students. The ostensible purpose is to encourage healthy sector growth, protect consumer interests, and prevent dishonest practices.

However, the regulators are extended arms of the Government and, hence, are not immune to political or other kinds of pressure. Plus, just like the Government, they tend to overreach. Controlling all aspects of business - from what you can sell to what you can advertise, how much you can charge and how much you can spend on what, what your service quality should be, and various other metrics. So, now, enterprises spend as much time submitting various 'Returns' to regulators as they spend growing their business. No one knows how these data are made use of.

But does regulation help? In my view, hardly. Despite regulation, banks accumulate NPAs, insurers lose value and fold up, stock market manipulation happens, Ponzi schemes come and go, buildings are not built in time, airlines go sick, and rotten films come to the theatre (are not film censors a regulation?).

One unstated risk of Government regulation (all regulations are government-ordained) is that the government starts 'underwriting' the risk against failure and inability to honour commitments. 'Since the Government has approved it, it should be safe'. The sovereign starts diluting itself to favour purely commercial enterprises with private money.

Let's look for less yet meaningful regulation rather than an overreaching parallel bureaucracy. Concentrate on a few cogent, well-defined, measurable metrics—the less you need, the better. Do not make information (except key metrics) mandatory to share for fear of non-compliance. Let the market play out, compete, and cooperate. '*Light touch regulation*' is the phrase.

A term often used in economics is '*Sunshine regulation.*' In other words, it informs the consumers and lets them decide.

Is not the market a better arbiter than a few people? Has God bestowed all the wisdom upon only a few government officials?

42

Hindi Hornet's Nest

When we study human language, we are approaching what some might call the 'human essence,' the distinctive qualities of the mind that are, so far as we know, unique to man.

- Noam Chomsky

In the comedy movie '*Wag the Dog*', a fictional war is created to divert the media's and people's attention from a sex scandal involving the President.

'Don't play with fire,' screams the DMK chief, and the TRP-hungry obliges with 'Breaking News'. This is despite the centre clarifying that the new educational policy is just a draft. It has withdrawn the portion related to the three-language formula, with Hindi being one of the languages, even from the draft circulated for public opinion.

'Not enough', thunders the chief. The agitation will gain momentum and could spiral out of control. Other southern nations would also join.

In fact, this is inherent in the 2019 mandate. Opposition parties have bagged seats only in the South of India or Bengal.

And you are already witnessing strident minority appeasement in Bengal (minorities 30 per cent, plus a massive influx of refugees from Bangladesh), with the CM overreacting to chants of 'Jai Sree Ram'.

If you recall, even after the 2014 verdict, linguistic agitation was launched on the UPSC issue, primarily by students with no academic credibility to make it to the finals. Very wisely, Arun Jaitley backed out. 'Linguistic emotions have potential of derailing government agenda on other issues', he said.

And this is precisely what the opposition wants. I suspect the parliament session will not be allowed to function. Anyway, the Indian parliament is meant not to function.

The ruling party base, mainly in the Hindi belt, is sure to react, exhorting the government to impose Hindi all over India. Most have never attempted to appreciate other Indian languages, and very few Indians are bilingual, anyway.

Media houses are already salivating at the prospect of a North-South divide, sparks, and a full-blown linguistic war. Nothing sells better than strife, and the TRP rating would touch sky-high.

We need to watch how the new Home Minister, known for his no-nonsense approach, will likely address this issue.

Ideally, there should be no language 'formula'. Children should be allowed to learn in the language of their parents' choice (and their own once they grow up). States should collaborate to produce books in different languages and provide teachers who can teach them. All other languages should be options—from other Indian languages to English, Chinese, Portuguese, Spanish, etc.

I am sure we have the wherewithal to create this infrastructure. Technology can help immensely here.

If you want to expand your chances of employment, learn new languages at your own expense. Indian states should collaborate to provide books, teachers, and other infrastructure in other states as part of 'cultural centres. ' Children and their parents are smart enough to learn new languages if it helps them further their education, career and overall growth. And if your state is making substantial economic progress, you may as well learn only your state language. Others would voluntarily learn your language.

But then, rational thinking and politics are oxymoronic.

P.S. This article was written before the current linguistic war in 2025

43

A Passage through Kolkata

Calcutta, if you must exile me, wound my lips before I go, only words remain and the gentle touch of your finger on my lips.
- Pritish Nandy

A visit to Kolkata is akin to reading a real-life Bangla classic. As your bus passes through places like Maniktala, Ulta Danga, Lal Bazaar, Tollygunz, Hazra, etc., pages from books written by greats such as Ishwarchandra Vidyasagar, Sharatchandra Chatterjee, Bankim Chandra Chatterjee, Rabindranath Tagore, Mahashweta Devi, Ashapoorna Devi, and countless others flash through your mind and heart.

With that, one starts living through the untold atrocities, famines, and sacrifices, the glorious era of the freedom movement, and the seminal contribution of Bengal's extraordinary men and women.

And you are also reminded, as if turning chapters of the book, of the pernicious practice ranging from sati, kulin pratha, child marriage, etc., and, again, the significant role played by the likes of Raja Rammohan Roy, Iswarchandra and many others to agitate for social reforms.

Yet another chapter of this virtual book reminds you about the spiritual quest, indeed the renaissance and reestablishment of Hinduism through the likes of Ramakrishna Paramhansa and Swami Vivekananda.

During my recent short trip through Kolkata, as I was turning through the pages and chapters of my virtual book of history, I did not miss that the city looked much cleaner. Everything - from road furniture to buildings - seemed to have been dyed in ubiquitous blue and white - the official colour of the ruling dispensation. Somehow, the Howrah Bridge escaped their attention.

There are also long overbridges - one after another - to reduce traffic congestion. Ubiquitous yellow Ambassador taxis proudly read 'No refusal', but it is more symbolic than any profound statement of intent. The new generation of Uber and Ola is playing on roads once ruled by communists.

And yes, there are many inexpensive Volvo buses. Imagine paying Rs 45 (USD 0.75) for a distance, for which *Namma Bangalore* (My Bangalore) easily fleeces you Rs 200.

Sadly, the trams seem to be in death throes - the only city with trams in India. What has not changed is the culture of *Bandh* (strike), ironically called by the ruling dispensation itself. Vestiges of a long communist rule, I guess. I experienced it first-hand.

To complete the story, Kolkata has the first metro in India, which is now being expanded through an under-river tunnel. A new metro station is coming up near the airport to connect it to the city.

The new airport terminal was spacious, clean, and well-managed. Howrah station was clean but as noisy as ever. But who would imagine clean eateries at Howrah offering a range of cuisine, including Flurry's bakery items? Seriously, that is some change. I recall, as a teenager, getting Typhoid after drinking adulterated cold drinks at Howrah station. The place resembled a dirty ghetto.

That brings me to its political dimension. Lots of us have a poor opinion of the ruling TMC and its mercurial leader, Mamata Banerjee. But she has delivered, right? Admittedly, the fruits of development have not reached far and wide, but they are in process.

The flagship of the PM program, *Swacch Bharat* (Clean India), has been implemented well in a state ruled by his bete noire.

The success of a clean India is evident everywhere. My friends who travelled to different parts of India over the recent vacation have come back with inspiring stories about citizen and government initiatives and how cleaner the places look now, from Rajasthan to Tamilnadu.

Except for Mumbai and Bangalore. These two places, ruled by opposite sides of the political spectrum—proving my political non-affiliation—have only gotten dirtier. Posh areas have open litter, overflowing gutters, and careless attitudes when maintaining our neighbourhood.

That is a pity. One is the financial capital of India, and the other is the IT hub. One is full of billionaires, and the other is full of cosmopolitan and sophisticated gentlemen who are rich, too. Both are full of people who have seen the world and have the correct ideas, means, and voices.

Something is missing. Unlike Kolkata, the citizens of Mumbai and Bengaluru are oblivious to their respective glorious books. Or, they have yet to take a leaf out of Kolkata's book in this respect.

44

Post Office

As a result of the digital age and the decline of first-class mail, there is no question that the Postal Service must change and develop a new business model.

- Bernie Sanders

I visited my local post office today for my annual investment ritual. The post office is quite spacious, and as I waited to be serviced, I looked around with mixed feelings.

On the positive side, I saw substantial computerisation at the front office. It had new swivel chairs, and much fewer paper files were strewn around, unlike in the past. I was informed that many services have moved online, and new services have been added, viz. packing services. Several process innovations have occurred, such as the passbook approach to issuing National Savings Certificates. New passbooks have been issued and linked to PAN (Tax ID) and Aadhar (Citizen ID).

But the office itself looked quite poorly equipped. There were loosely hanging wires, no backup power to run fans and lights, gum marks left behind by numerous stickers and notices, and a worn-out wooden bench for waiting customers. I wondered if the office looked welcoming to its customers and if the employees felt motivated enough to come to their office every day and felt comfortable being there throughout the day.

I also realised that changes are coming too fast for the customers, many of them senior citizens. They looked confused. Happily, there were other younger customers to help them out.

Post offices all over the world provide critical services. POS banks are pretty popular. The banking and insurance services (as underwriters or corporate agents) of India Post have been underutilised. Technology has killed many of the services offered by posts and telegraphs, including telegraphic services, money transfer services, etc. With private courier agencies being much more hungry for business, the mainstay of the postal services has taken a hit.

I reckon India Post has suffered from a lack of vision, leadership, and innovation—a picture of overall neglect. India Post has over 150,000 post offices, many of which are in deep hinterlands. It is a well-established infrastructure just waiting to be tapped.

Postal services are essentially logistical services, delivering physical goods from producers to consumers and from consumers to consumers. While all value-added services are interesting, they are not the postal services' core offering or strength.

Oddly, logistics has become much more critical in the digital age of e-tailing. E-tailers must deliver fast, over more significant landmasses, and with assurance of timeliness. Yet, most deliveries today are through private agencies and contract employees. India Post has a ready opportunity to tap into this vast (and growing) potential.

Several summers back, I conducted a workshop for India Post at a prestigious business school. We were creating mock business plans. I suggested that India Post should look at its core competency. I hazarded a guess that services such as money transfer, banking, intermediation, communications, and investment management are not its core offering. Many of these may not exist in their current form and nature. Maybe I was partly right.

45

Public Construction

—♡—

Building is not just about shelter. It's about realizing dreams, making statements, creating spaces where life happens.
- John "Architect" Aarons

I worked on a project in Germany many mild summers and frigid winters ago. This large IT hub housed several office blocks in the middle of a vast expanse of farmlands, touching the borders of a minor, beautiful village. Civilisation ended there, as a thick forest started immediately thereafter.

I found the car parks fascinating. Almost invisible to my eyes (I am used to behemoth concrete jungles), multi-level car parks were nicely tucked between the jungle and office blocks. They were nothing more than three-inch concrete blocks supported by metal pillars, none very thick and imposing. And, of course, ramps to take your car to the upper floors. There were no walls, wires, glass, or ugly, invasive advertisement boards.

It was just functional. It was invisible and did not impede the view of the lovely ambience.

I often wondered whether it was strong enough, whether it was really concrete, and whether the iron pillars were made of some very special material. Of course, they were. But technology exists to make things that are strong but not imposing in dimensions.

I had a similar impression of the road overbridge over the Autobahn for pedestrians and light vehicles. It was light, aesthetically designed, supported by wires, and had flower pots along its entire length. The public toilets were small, cute, and functional, melting into the surroundings.

Come to India: Mumbai, Bangalore, and other places are witnessing public construction at a maddening pace. Leave aside new airports - admittedly of high standards - and look at foot over-bridges, road and rail over bridges, public car parks, toilet blocks, and housing blocks. A case in point is the Bangalore metro, which is overground even in the most important and beautiful streets like M.G. Road.

So much concrete, bricks, and iron go into it. I suspect someone is more interested in creating a place for advertisement boards than the utility itself. They have no concern about aesthetics. And it takes ages to build walls, pour concrete, and paint them. The finish is usually poor. Degradation is quick.

Why can we not innovate, experiment, and consider the city's beauty? Are our universities and institutions incapable of designing, testing and recommending lovely designs? Can we not get ideas from the world?

46
Police System

The police are not here to create disorder; they are here to preserve disorder.
- Richard J. Daley

As a kid, I grew up being disciplined in the name of the "red-capped policeman". Eat, or else the red-capped policeman will come. Sleep, else...

After growing up, on inquiry, I gathered that even my parental generation was threatened in the name of police viz—pre-independence police, wearing loose khaki half-pants and wielding a danda.

I see, even today, children are disciplined in the name of 'khaki-clad' police. I am unsure if children in other parts of the world are disciplined in the name of cops.

So, this must be the most enduring threat - spanning four generations.

Why should it be so? Why does our heartbeat increase when we see a cop?

Accept it. The lower-level police chap is mighty. He has power without responsibility, unlike the seniors who have authority but are answerable.

Remember that joke about a blind woman thanking the DGP for helping her cross the road and wishing him a promotion to become a Thanedar?

If a constable misbehaves with you or even beats you up, you can do precious little. What can you do? Go to higher-ups? They have better things to worry about. Go to court? It will take several decades to decide.

I have had to go to the police station a few times to register complaints about lost cell phones (to prevent misuse) or something like that. I can tell you, every time I come back bruised. The ambience is unwelcome - you are an intruder in their daily life. One aspect you cannot miss observing is that the police station is a depressing workplace, and extended duty hours away from family are not adding to the morale and competency of the men in Khaki.

Much has been written about police reforms, but very little has been done. More has been written about intelligence gathering, using technology, and separating policing from prosecution. We only hear about law and order being a state subject. And it ends there.

I know one thing. No constable is recruited on merit - physique, stamina, education, sport, etc. It is all based on how much you can pay and whom you know.

In this scenario, Return on Investment (ROI) counts. And allegiance matters.

What happens in Basirhat, Azamgarh, or any other place, for that matter, reflects this reality. The police lack competence and are there to get ROI and pander to their masters.

47

Farmer's Suicide

If agriculture goes wrong, nothing else will have a chance to go right.
- M. S. Swaminathan

Let us talk about the agrarian crisis, especially farmers' suicides.

Now, please do not ask me what do I know about agriculture.

Well, I do not go beyond my kitchen garden. But relax. This account is from a person who has done an extensive field survey on this topic as part of an NGO (Non-Government Organisation). I am only relaying.

We all know about farmers' suicides. Despite farm loan waivers, there has not been a downward trend in suicide cases.

Have farmers been committing suicide forever? NO. There is hardly any evidence of mass farmer suicide before the last 30 to 40 years, except as isolated events.

What has changed? Farmers have always been poor, permanently indebted, and troubled by moneylenders.

And the poorest farmers and marginal labourers never received loans. Only those with some assets could get a loan—house, land, etc.

One significant change has been the adoption of better seeds (not GM—it is not widespread except for BT cotton). Better seeds need more water, more fertilisers, etc. But if the yield were not commensurate, farmers would not embrace them. They have centuries of wisdom.

So, what else?

This expert says that it is the pesticides.

More and more chemical pesticides are being sprayed now. Worse still, with hardly any personal protection. The farmers ingest them through breathing, skin, and, sometimes, food—a small quantity at a time, but throughout the farming cycle.

Many pesticides used in India are banned worldwide.

Many of these pesticides are known to cause mood changes and depression.

Now, you have a clue.

Of course, more empirical evidence needs to be collected and analysed to prove the hypothesis that certain insecticides cause depression, and these, more than any other single cause, if not handled properly by trained doctors, could lead to suicidal tendencies.

P.S. Medical research can reach strange conclusions. Did you read about the research that found that children in parts of Bihar were dying during the summer months due to a bizarre and sudden illness caused by consuming litchi of good quality, especially on an empty stomach?

48
Saving Our Weavers

I am the weaver of Thy Name
Surat and nirat are the two pegs
That hold the frame of my loom ;
Thus, I weave with care and discernment
The cloth of Thy Name.
- Saint Kabir Das

During last weekend's trip to the temple town of Udupi (coastal Karnataka, India) to meet a friend, Rajeev Bhattathiripad, and for pilgrimage, we had a chance to visit Udupi Weaver's Cooperative to purchase a few handloom sarees.

During the conversation, we gathered that for each handloom saree selling for around Rs 600 (USD 9.00), the weaver makes only Rs 100 (USD 1.50), which could be one day's earnings, given the time it takes to hand weave a 5.50-meter length of cotton saree.

No wonder handloom units have shut down over the years—from 700 to a mere 20 looms are operating now at Udupi. Since the younger generation is looking for greener urban pastures and alternate professions, the looms are run by ageing weavers, whose productivity is even lower—they make just Rs 50 daily. Many of them are in the clutches of moneylenders. It presents a stark picture of rural indebtedness and penury.

This glorious tradition shall disappear altogether within a generation or two. This shall be replaced by power loom-made or factory-made clothes spun in large quantities - all of uniform quality, bereft of any individuality or character. Maybe it will be made in China!

The problem is common to weavers and all artisans who use their age-old skills to create artefacts that reflect our distinct culture and connect us with our past. The wooden toy manufacturers of Chennapatna, Karnataka, find it challenging to compete with imported Chinese plastic or mechanical toys, which typically cost a third of wooden toys.

What should have happened, ideally, is that, as consumers, we should have patronised and encouraged to purchase handmade stuff. But we are far too much driven by price - not only the lower middle class but also those who can afford it. For example, the saree, which sells for Rs 600, should have been priced upwards of Rs 1500 to make weaving attractive. But, at that price point, there would be no takers.

Weavers should be encouraged to create value-added offerings with contemporary designs to make their products appealing to the younger generation. After all, the saree itself is going out of fashion. Admittedly, some efforts are underway, for example, ladies' tops, kurtas, etc., but it is too late. A focused attempt to revitalise our handloom and all man-made artefacts is needed to prevent the rural economy from complete ruin.

My second reflection was that our generation could be the last to visit and contribute to running temples. These remind us of our childhood and help us connect with our past.

How long will this continue? At the risk of sweeping generalisation, the younger generation is not interested in religion, culture, or temple visits. When they grow up, will they contribute to temple upkeep, or will these magnificent traditions shall decay for want of financing? And with that shall disappear a piece of our being? Ditto is for our traditional architecture, culture, and age-old traditions.

I may be exaggerating. They may take better care of their heritage than we could. They may bring technology and stronger institutions together. Material well-being, spiritual well-being, and an attempt to reconnect with the past may herald a new Indian Renaissance.

You can see green shoots of this already: online handicraft promotions, growing interest in Khadi fashion, attempts to connect with weavers directly, and disintermediation by some well-meaning youth.

In the 1957 movie Naya Daur (New Era), a fascinating race occurs between a Tonga (a horse-driven chariot) and a newly introduced bus service. The bus loses, and its service is withdrawn. Tonga, which represents village self-sufficiency and rural jobs, wins.

It was just a movie made over sixty years ago. We need the Tonga to win again, not by participating in a nerve-wracking race involving a poor beast and a machine, but by all of us reflecting and caressing the beast gently and consciously taking the slower path to the villages.

That shall be an authentic tribute to Mahatma Gandhi. And to Shayar Sahir Ludhiyanavi, whose birthday falls this week and who wrote in 1958

वो सुबह कभी तो आयेगी, वो सुबह कभी तो आयेगी
इन काली सदियों के सर से, जब रात का आंचल ढलकेगा
जब अम्बर झूम के नाचेगी, जब धरती नग़मे गाएगी
वो सुबह कभी तो आयेगी ...

जिस सुबह की खातिर जुग-जुग से,
हम सब मर-मर के जीते हैं
जिस सुबह की अमृत की धुन में, हम ज़हर के प्याले पीते हैं
इन भूखी प्यासी रूहों पर, एक दिन तो करम फ़रमायेगी
वो सुबह कभी तो आयेगी ...

माना के अभी तेरे मेरे इन अरमानों की, कीमत कुछ नहीं
मिट्टी का भी है कुछ मोल मगर,
इनसानों की कीमत कुछ भी नहीं
इनसानों की इज़्ज़त जब झूठे सिक्कों में ना तोली जायेगी
वो सुबह कभी तो आयेगी ...

बीतेंगे कभी तो दिन आखिर, ये भूख और बेकारी के
टूटेंगे कभी तो बुत आखिर, दौलत की इजारेदारी की
अब एक अनोखी दुनिया की, बुनियाद उठाई जायेगी
वो सुबह कभी तो आयेगी ...

मजबूर बुढ़ापा जब सूनी, राहों में धूल न फेंकेगा
मासूम लड़कपन जब गंदी, गलियों में भीख ना माँगेगा
हक माँगने वालों को, जिस दिन सूली न दिखाई जायेगी
वो सुबह कभी तो आयेगी ...

That morning will surely come, that morning will surely come,
When the dark centuries will fade, and night's veil will be undone.
When the skies will dance in glee, when the earth will sing in harmony,
That morning will surely come...

For that morning we've lived and died for, through ages and despair,
In search of its nectar, we've drunk poison with despair.
On these hungry, thirsty souls, mercy will shine one day,
That morning will surely come...
True, right now, our dreams may not have much worth,
Even earth has some value, but humans seem of no mirth.
When human dignity is not measured in coins so hollow,
That morning will surely come...
One day, the days of hunger and despair will surely end,
The idols of wealth will break, and the monopoly will bend.
A new world will rise with a foundation so bold,
That morning will surely come...
When the forced old age will not scatter dust on the roads,
When childhood will no longer beg in the alleys with loads,
Those who demand their rights, on that day will not be crucified,
That morning will surely come...

49
Second Charkha Revolution

⎯⎯⎯❧⎯⎯⎯

Khadi stands for simplicity, not shoddiness. It sits well on the shoulders
of the poor, and it can be made, as it was made in the days of the yore,
to adorn the bodies of the richest and the most artistic men and women.
It is reviving ancient art and crafts.
- Mahatma Gandhi

The new uniform of Marshals at Rajya Sabha has raised eyebrows, and justifiably so.

The change requests came from the Marshals, as it took too long to tie the turban. To my untrained eyes, it reminded me of the British Raj legacy, which only a few institutions refused to give up - Marshals at the Indian Parliament, servers at an Indian coffee house and a few old institutions like SBI (State Bank of India), where coffee and tea are still brought by the guys in turban for the Chairman and his guests. (My British friends were shocked to see the Raj tradition still being followed in India).

You may even ask why we need Marshals. That's a good question. But it has created some employment, at least.

The new uniform seemed to suggest a military takeover of Rajya Sabha, with soldiers flanking the hapless Vice President. If you observe closely, the uniform colour is closer to that of security guards at IT companies.

It is not fair to the Marshals, the August house and the honourable members of the house.

Why not go for Indian attire? Like a nice crisp khadi white pyjama kurta with a khadi bandi? It would look contemporary and very Indian and would align well with the politicians who, anyway, mostly wear Khadi.

It may be replaced on specific occasions by a dress representing different states. Why not? Rajya Sabha is a house of states. For example, *Vesti* (long loincloth) to replace Pyjama...

Let us not stop here. The entire production of pure khadi clothes (Charkha upwards) is employment-intensive, brings revenue down to the villages (cutting across religious lines), and can reignite (and reimagine) the cottage industry. It is very Indian, very Gandhian, and wonderful.

And it is most suitable for the Indian climate. Ask any fashion designer.

So, why not make it mandatory for our representatives to wear only khadi at legislatures and public functions and encourage government offices to adopt these? Or, for that matter, school uniforms? Let us be proud of something made in India by Indians with their own hands.

We should promote khadi everywhere government funds are available, except for the armed and civil forces.

Do you think khadi is boring? Trust me, you get fantastic variety, especially for women. And it is not restricted to only kurta, pyjama, and dhoti. You have handmade silk, too, for occasions.

Try it, and you may start loving the experience.

50

Productivity Gain

If you have men who will exclude any of God's creatures from the shelter of compassion and pity, you will have men who will deal likewise with their fellow men.

- Francis of Assisi

A set of researchers carried out very interesting (and even poignant, in my view) research on the tea pluckers in the North Eastern hills of India.

They checked their eyesight and gave them power glasses costing Rs. 200 each.

They measured their productivity again and found that productivity had gone up significantly. Those above age 40 showed an over 20% increase in plucking, and those over age 50 showed a staggering 30% gain in productivity.

This was not the 'Hawthorne effect' (a celebrated case where mere attention leads to increased productivity). Tea plucking requires a high level of hand-eye coordination, and, shockingly, their employers were apathetic to this simple step to boost productivity. Increased productivity helps all - the tea garden owners, above all. It also increases income for pluckers, and their children can possibly study rather than being plucked (pun intended) halfway to start working in tea gardens.

But, there is a broader point I am making. There are low-hanging fruits to boost productivity. Better tools, health checks, hygienic food, clean drinking water, better working environment...

Rather than discussing productivity ad nauseam on TV and in seminars, one needs to pay attention to small things. It does not cost much to treat your resources as human beings. But the benefits are enormous, even from the narrow capitalistic greed angle.

51
Nation of Renters

The biggest risk is not taking any risk... In a world that is changing really quickly, the only strategy that is guaranteed to fail is not taking risks.

- Mark Zuckerberg

'*Living off the Earth*'. Usually, we use this adage for the farmers. But, farmers, irrespective of geography, are very industrious, enterprising and risk-takers.

There is another class that lives off the Earth: the urban landholders, especially those with parcels of land in vantage locations. Many would have inherited it, many others would have bought it at the right time, and the price has appreciated.

In a rather uncharitable comment, many urban land holdings date back to the British period, when rulers granted favours to obedient servants of the Raj. And who were they?

So, what do you do if you have a parcel of land that suddenly has appreciated in value?

You give it to a builder who constructs apartments or villas. You get roughly 40 to 50% of the built-up area, which you can sell off and enjoy the proceeds for the rest of your life.

If the land is on a busy street, you construct a shop or two - sometimes several floors - higher ones for commercial or residential use. In most places, little attention is paid to aesthetics, design or safety. Essentially, it saves on the architect's cost. When it's finished, start to look to rent it out to shops and showrooms. Or seek assistance from real estate brokers who thrive on information asymmetry.

Look carefully. In most cases, only the ground floor is rented. Sadly, the upper floors have no takers, with a fading '*To let*' board hanging. The landholders would have taken a big loan to construct this piece.

You would be surprised at the churn of shops and showrooms if you have keen eyes. Investments are made in interiors, and shops open with considerable fanfare. After a year or so, the shutters are down. Why?

I suspect rentals are too high, and there is insufficient footfall and demand, as many shops sell the same stuff. And customers are moving to malls and mobiles.

Some landowners take shortcuts. They simply put pillars and plates, create a basement and a lift shaft, and peddle it as a '*Warm Shell*'. You do the rest of it and pay a fat rent.

Some go a step further and offer land as '*Build to Suit*'. You construct, use it, and, at the end of a certain period, give it to the owners. BOT model...

Why am I writing all these? I worry that we have become a nation of low-risk takers who look for the easy way out. There is not much innovation, not enough enterprising, and not enough attempts to produce new ideas and new goods.

We are content following the beaten track.

Unless the nation innovates, people will take risks and break away from the beaten track; we will only remain nations of lessors, lessees, and shops peddling products manufactured in China and the Far East.

52

Photography Prohibited

The camera makes everyone a tourist in other people's reality, and eventually in one's own.
- Susan Sontag

'Photography Prohibited'

How often do you see this board at places of tourist interest in India?

I am more than disappointed; I am intrigued.

Photography is free publicity. Tourists take selfies and pictures, post them on social media, share them with friends, and generate curiosity and enquiry, which could lead to higher footfall and boost the local economy.

Why stop photographing tourist places? No such bar exists for capturing images of poverty, squalor, or tragedy. As a result, more negative news and images circulate than images of incredible temple architecture, mountains, engineering marvels, and other things we could be proud of. In any case, media, intellectuals, NGOs, and liberal thinkers leave no stone unturned in portraying us negatively.

Why should photography be banned? At the Somnathpura temple (an exquisite piece of stone carvings and temple architecture) near Bangalore, the security guard informed us that photography is forbidden to prevent Pakistanis from targeting their missiles at the temple. Now, why should someone deploy a long-range ballistic missile to destroy a non-functioning derelict temple? Are we not doing a fine job of destroying our heritage by scribbling our names on the walls?

In Maharashtra, a colleague of mine got in trouble after clicking a picture of his friends against the backdrop of a bridge. The policeman demanded to see the image and 'take necessary action'. In a panic, my friend deleted the photo. The policeman was annoyed at the 'destruction of evidence' and threatened with action. What action? Incarcerate the person for the rest of his life?

The most common excuse is for security reasons. This is bunkum. First, more detailed pictures and topography are available through satellite imagery. Second, Google Maps provides more detailed directions to the place than any human reconnaissance. Finally, to a determined person with a sinister design, it is very easy to carry a spy cam. Even visual inspection is good enough if one gains access to the place.

The second reason is to protect the object from degradation. The Mona Lisa is the most photographed picture - only flash is prohibited.

And then, the conservative excuse of 'prevent nuisance' by trigger-happy youngsters, who would not concentrate on the beauty of the place. Come on, accept the generational change. If someone has taken out time and is spending money, they have full right to enjoy their way. So long as one does not come in the way of someone else's devotion or enjoyment.

Otherwise, the generation will ignore the architectural marvel and head to shopping malls.

All tourist and religious places should be thrown open for photography and videography.

53

Financial Fraudsters

Rather fail with honor than succeed by fraud.
- Sophocles

There is an old R K Laxman cartoon in which the policeman, on the chase of a history-sheeter, suddenly stops in his tracks. The caption reads, '*The fellow has moved into the next Thana zone.*'

Sadly, it is true today.

For long, drug peddlers, criminals, and smugglers have exploited the loopholes in international law and the fact that despite all bilateral agreements, extradition is extremely cumbersome, time-consuming and painful.

Remember Charles Shobraj? A wanted criminal in several countries, he continued to evade capital punishment and continued to live (and got married). Or Chota Rajan? Or, for that matter, Abu Salem, who was finally extradited from Portugal on the assurance that he would not be awarded a death sentence. Remember, he committed a heinous crime in India, not Portugal. Yes, Indian law is not to be applied.

It does not matter that the drug lords run their business globally and render a dark, painful and wretched future for youth across the globe. Yet, the international community has not come together for a speedy handover of drug smugglers, except if it is a mighty nation like the USA.

It's a slightly different story for terrorists. One country's terrorists could be another country's freedom fighters. And then there are 'good' and 'bad' terrorists. Scores of wanted Indian terrorists have found haven in Pakistan.

But, pray tell me, who gains by sheltering Tiger Memon or Dawood Ibrahim? They do not have even a 'K' in their name. What about scores of Khalistanis enjoying hospitality in Canada and plotting their sinister design to break India?

What about financial fraudsters? It is now a sickening pattern that Indian fraudsters slip out of the country in the nick of time. They receive timely tips, help from equally corrupt people, and 'ease of escaping through swanky new airports and liberal immigration control'. They travel first class with dozens of suitcases. On their way out, they receive a gravity-defying bow and sickening genuflection from the awe-struck, obsequious airport and airline staff. Lalit Modi, Vijay Mallya, and Nirav Modi are just a few of these names. Once they go to another country, they find a safe and welcoming haven overseas. Extradition, if at all possible, is time-consuming.

Who gains by their presence in the UK or the USA? If they add to your economy or create jobs there, please host them by all means. But a crook shall remain a crook, irrespective of the geography of operations. And do remember, these fraudsters have decamped with the hard-earned money of millions of poor Indians. And your fraudsters, too, can decamp.

The so-called long arm of the law is not that long. The moment it tries to reach the fraudsters who have taken shelter in another nation, the judiciary grabs the arm and says, '*Your thana area ends, dude*' (Your territory ends, dear).

So, every current or future fraudster would have a plan B ready: Escape to another nation. A nation that is not on good terms with your country, a nation where the judicial system is slow and corrupt, or a nation where the judiciary is so mired in rules and fairness that it is oblivious to the big international picture. And you can afford to hire the most expensive lawyers with their loot. Also, humans are mortal.

No wonder, '*Don ko gyarah mulkon ki pulis dhundh rahi hai*' (police of 11 nations are searching for Don. A popular dialogue from a Hindi movie)

The time has come when the nations come together on at least financial fraudsters and hand the fraudsters over quickly so that '*They are brought to justice.*'

54
The Fractured Himalaya

India Conquered and dominated China culturally for 20 centuries without ever having to send a single soldier across her border.
- Hu Shih

Having read unhealthy and toxic posts on social media about China's treachery and PM Nehru's folly leading to the Indo-China war and India's defeat, I picked up the book ' *The Fractured Himalaya*' by ex-Foreign Secretary Ms Nirupama Rao to gain a deeper insight into this complex issue.

The book covers the period 1949 to 1962 and masterfully narrates the events as they unfolded between India, China, and Tibet.

I found the book so engrossing that several times, I paused to look at the net to find details about and see pictures of the politicians, diplomats, and other protagonists alluded to in this rather voluminous book.

Ms Rao did a lot of research and talked to scores of people from the era and afterwards before starting to write this book, which is more of a study than easy reading. However, to keep an average reader glued in, she shared interesting anecdotes that make readers read up and explore further.

Yes, it is true that Nehru invested a lot of bandwidth in improving relations with China. And yes, he did promote China's entry into the United Nations (the PRC only got entry in 1971), believing that China's isolation needs to end for a better world order. It can be forcefully argued that some or many of our present-day problems stem from China's prominent role and veto power at the United Nations.

In a way, the author argues that India and China were two different worlds. One was a fledging democracy committed to nonviolence, peace, and a liberal outlook that trusted in traditional and historical boundaries. India was cautious about precipitating boundary issues with her neighbour, trusted China's words, and believed in good-neighbourly relations between giant Asians.

Others looked at the boundary as strategic. They were deeply lacerated by and, therefore, bitter and suspicious of imperial powers, their legacy, and Shenanigans. China was also looking to expand its revolutionary ideas.

Perhaps Nehru was hemmed in by his convictions, seeking a global leadership position and a vision of international order. However, his diplomats and bureaucrats did not serve him well. They could not offer the proper perspective or caution about China's intentions. A nascent nation with a modest economy could not adequately invest military power to counter China. The result is for all to see.

A fractured polity led to inflexibility on border issues. Belligerence in parliament and among the people made Nehru harden his stand, leading to a disastrous war.

But as they say, the past is another country. We would be served well if we learned from the past and showed firmness but flexibility in dealing with our neighbours. And yes, empty words have no meaning in international relations. Prevarication and one-sided assumptions mean nothing.

Overall, this was an excellent and insightful read. It has kindled my interest in exploring China's history from ancient times.

55

Chronicles and Illusion of Peace

People who ask us when we will hold talks with Pakistan are perhaps not aware that over the last 55 years, every initiative for a dialogue with Pakistan has invariably come from India.
- Atal Bihari Vajpayee

I just completed reading this fascinating and insightful book, '*Spy Chronicles and Illusion of Peace*'.

The book has received lots of controversial coverage, as it is based on the conversation by author Aditya Sinha with AS Dulat, Former RAW chief and Asad Durrani, former ISI Chief.

You will be disappointed if you are looking for 'Spy vs. Spy' or the revelation of classified information. Both spy chiefs are first-class professionals dedicated to their profession and their nation. Besides, they are bound by a lifelong oath of secrecy.

I suspect the entire controversy was manufactured to boost sales. We are living in different times.

However, this does not diminish the book's profundity or, more importantly, its intent.

The book is written in a guided conversation style in which the spy chiefs speak frankly about various issues, people, and controversies.

I don't want to summarise the conversation, but I think it's insightful to draw a few conclusions.

1) Conversation and even cooperation at the highest level are continuous processes, notwithstanding high-pitched acerbic exchanges of words and emotional media hysteria.

2) There are enough people on either side who want peace and see the dividends peace shall offer to the people and the world.

3) It is generally believed that gradualism is the right approach rather than a Big Bang solution. Small gains, continuous exchanges, and reviews are suggested rather than a time-bound, goal-oriented approach.

4) There is a general realisation that the Kashmir border cannot be redrawn, and Balochistan cannot be wrested away. However, these key issues are getting in the way of sorting out minor issues—low-hanging fruits that can benefit both nations: trade across the border (rather than through UAE), cultural exchange, and a few such issues.

5) Despite the animosity, soldiers and intelligence professionals greatly respect one another. Even during war, out of vulnerability, the exchanges have been mainly on military targets.

6) Yet, there is enough at stake for the powers on each side to keep the situation simmering. This helps nations get aid, keeps international focus on them, and keeps people busy away from key development issues.

7) Interestingly, Pakistan expected retaliation from India after significant events such as the Parliament attack and Pathankot. Sharp, short, and limited exchanges help deflect public anger on either side and are manufactured mainly by both sides to handle domestic outrage. Pakistan was surprised that our response was so muted.

As a kid, I remember Philip Bobb writing about India-Pakistan relations. He wrote that India-Pakistan relations cannot get very close, as the wounds of partition are not fully healed. And they cannot get too bad, as there is enough in common between them, including people on either side.

The spy chiefs, whose primary job was to collect information, analyse these and, at times, foment trouble (and relish trouble), want to see the irrelevance of the border - in fact, a confederation. It's interesting to hear Asad Durrani talk about Akhand Bharat - a right-winger's term - and how it is possible without altering borders.

56
Everyone Loves a Good Drought

When a poor person dies of hunger, it has not happened because God did not take care of him or her. It has happened because neither you nor I wanted to give that person what he or she needed.
- Mother Teresa

I read this excellent book, '*Everyone Loves a Good Drought*' by P Sainath.

This highly acclaimed and award-winning book is a compilation of articles by this Magsaysay-awarded journalist that appeared in The Times of India during the eighties and nineties.

The book revolves around stories of the poor, marginalised, tribal, remote, and exploited sections of India. He has covered a few districts in Bihar, MP, Orissa, and Tamilnadu to highlight people's plights there.

So, there is a bizarre story of an administrative experiment intended to increase the milk yield of local cows. In this experiment, local bulls are castrated, and artificial insemination is carried out with imported semen. The calves did not survive, and the genre of local bulls was lost forever.

There are stories of tribal medical practitioners and quacks who administer intravenous saline for all or any ailment simply for the awe it creates and the money it can make.

There are also stories of nonexistent schools or the headmaster taking the attendance register home to mark his daily presence in school from the comfort of his home. Of course, he would have filled out several leave applications with blank dates and left them with a local confidant—just in case of an inspection.

Or the tragedy of forced displacement in the name of progress, in the form of dams, mines or factories - the benefit of which never reaches the local populace.

Or the usury, forcing the poor to sell produce at a fraction of market price, taking small loans from local money lenders at interest rates ranging between 120% to 360% per annum, forced to buy their daily needs from the same local guy, mortgaging their land parcel (and losing it) and working as forced labour for generations. There are stories of migration to big cities, child labour and also sexual exploitation. It also covers the much-publicised case of the sale of girls by family members.

Or the shenanigans of local distilleries, who can use any material they can lay their hands on to ferment and brew intoxicants. And how they are protected by the powers that be.

Or, for that matter, local police and administrators, who let no opportunity go by to extract small bribes and cuts from the hapless.

And untold corruption in the form of relief work. The corrupt and those in hand and gloves call it the third crop.

The book is full of real-life anecdotes about how development has not reached the poor and needy and how they are exploited, alienated, and sacrificed at the altar of development.

The author argues that while we learn about episodes, we miss structural infirmities, which render the poor and weak at the margin of survival, and a small incidence, like an outbreak of Cholera, is enough to wipe them out.

The role of the press and journalists has also been highlighted, as they have scant concern for the poor, look only for catchy headlines, do very little fieldwork in remote areas, and depend on official machinery for news.

Of course, there are stories of fightbacks, seminal work done by individuals, small groups, and a few committed administrators, and the ennobling stories of art, poetry, painting, games, etc., of the tribals, marginalised, and the poor.

My reflection for the day is: Why do millions continue to be on the margin in a free, welfare-oriented democracy, in a land with bountiful rains, abundant sunshine, amazing landscapes, and immeasurable natural resources—including minerals?

And I realise, shockingly, that democracy itself may be responsible for some of our ills.

If you imagine the entire population as a familiar, bell-shaped statistical curve, most live within a few standard deviations from the centre (mean). Some are extremely rich and have carved out a world of their own. And some are extremely poor, vulnerable and weak - the other extreme of the bell curve.

With development, the mean shifts, but the variance does not (Development economists call it an improvement in per capita income, but the Gini index, measuring inequality, does not improve). The extremely poor remain at the margin. And since they are in the minority, the engine of democracy does not worry about them—they do not influence the outcome of the dance of democracy called elections. They are the true minorities.

Most often, we refer to religious minorities. But there are also environmental minorities (who pay the price of damage to the ecosystem and global warming), geographic minorities (living in remote and inaccessible areas), ethnic minorities (tribals), demographic minorities (very old), and so on.

Unlike religious minorities, who are more concentrated in some areas and could affect the outcome of elections, other minorities are, more often, scattered. Worse still, you could be on different sides of the divide along various fault lines - a geographic minority could be the beneficiary of environmental degradation in some cases. Where will your loyalty lie?

Democracy is an expensive institution - you need money to promote yourself and highlight your achievements. And this money is more likely to come from the oppressors than the oppressed. They have an entrenched interest in keeping the current order going on. Less is the achievement; more is the need for promotion and acquiring a support base - more is the dependence on the moneyed and the need to pander to their needs rather than that of the weak and scattered.

Meanwhile, people experiencing poverty can wait.

For, have we not been told that

'They also serve those who stand and wait.'

And that *'The poor and weak shall inherit the kingdom of heaven.'*

57

Privatisation of Necessities

When there is no middle class, and the poor greatly exceed in number, troubles arise, and the state soon comes to an end.

- Aristotle

As kids, we could surreptitiously enter a friend's house and startle him with a '*Bhow Wow*'. It was great fun and was possible, as the doors were always open and welcoming. Today, kids must enter details in the security log, announce the visit, and pass through CCTV before arriving at the friend's door. Trust is lost. We seem to be overdoing / overcorrecting.

It also underscores the level of private intervention in areas which were traditionally the state's domain and responsibility.

'*Security*'. It manifests everywhere.

We used to drink tap water at our playground. Today, we need bottled water, UV, or RO filter water.

There are no public places to swim anymore in big cities.

Communities have started building connecting roads and appointing private agencies to clean areas and collect refuse.

We do not trust the electric supply or its quality and depend on our power sources, such as DG sets and inverters.

The state-run hospitals and subsidised medicines have given way to the greed of private hospitals, for whom you are a '*customer*' and a '*business opportunity.*'

We are told that the air we breathe is unhealthy, so we should have air filters.

Gradually, the state is receding, and private enterprises are rising—even in areas that were once the domain of the state.

And it ensures unequal distribution, even of fundamental necessities of life.

A brave new world? Or a scary new order?

58
The Great Game

<hr>

There is no hunting like the hunting of man, and those who have hunted armed men long enough and liked it, never care for anything else thereafter.
- Ernest Hemingway

'Un-put-downable'.

This is the word I texted to a friend, who recommended the excellent book '*The Great Game*' by British Journalist Peter Hopkirk. Interestingly, the phrase 'The Great Game' is attributed to Rudyard Kipling in his book Kim, but it was coined more than a century ago by a British soldier spy.

This book, published in 1990, is based on years of research by the author. It covers the eighteenth and nineteenth centuries, ending towards the beginning of the twentieth century against the backdrop of Central Asia of the period.

Part of it is the power struggle between Tzarsit Russia and Victorian England, who wanted to expand their territories, covering Turkey, Iran, Afghanistan, Mongolia, Caucasus, Baltic, Pamirs, present-day Pakistan, Tibet, and China. I have missed many names.

The power struggle arose as the English, having established themselves in India—the jewel in their royal crown—were paranoid about Russian expansionist designs. And, indeed, ambitious Russians were keen to do so.

Add to this the lack of maps, unchartered territories, inaccessible regions, extreme climate, hostile people, poor transport (horse was the principal means) and barbaric regimes—even cannibals. This book is essentially a British account by an author who seems unhappy with the British policy of masterly inactivity. No wonder the Indian mutiny is mentioned in passing, and the opium war in China (which could embarrass the British) is dismissed as having no relevance to the narrative.

One-upmanship involved soldiers on either side trying to charter territories, moving around in disguise, and befriending rulers in places like Iran, Afghanistan, Khanates of central Asia, Bokhara, Kyiv, Ashgar, Tashkent, Samarkand, etc., and palace intrigues, treachery, war, counterplots, cooperation, chivalry, risk-taking, and exemplary bravery and patriotism.

There were innovations such as gifting horses to Maharaja Ranjit Singhji, which the British carried in a barge over the Indus to chart the river and something similar up the Oxus River in Central Asia by Russians.

Not to talk of brave warriors such as Gurkhas, Sikhs, Turkmans, Cozzaks, Uzbeks and Pathans.

The book is fascinating as it covers a geography few of us have read about in schools or thereafter. It is about a period when new war technologies were coming into being, such as new transport, viz. Railways were being laid, and spy vs spy was an absolute top-class terrestrial affair.

The book provides a wonderful period account and also provides a glimpse into the minds of the nationalities involved—indeed, their psyches to this day.

Written in effortless styles, such as *'If you were to pass through Bokhara, you would have seen a strange sight of a European getting into an Armenian dress..'*

Highly recommended, but a thick 600-page book.

In the end, one often wonders over two questions that have caused angst to me for ages.

1) How could a handful of English capture and rule an ancient, wise, rich nationality like India for over two centuries?

2) More disturbingly, except for the change in global order and values, what has changed since then to prevent its repeat today?

59
Angela's Ashes

I read this profoundly moving book, 'Angela's Ashes', by Irish American School teacher Frank McCourt.

This Pulitzer prize-winning tragicomic memoir, which is also the plot of a major motion picture, deals with the author's early life in the USA and then Limerick, Ireland, and is set in the nineteen thirties and forties. It covers his impecunious childhood days, where his father is an Irish alcoholic, and his mother runs the household on church doles and, occasionally, begging. The author witnesses the death of siblings owing to hunger and malnourishment and is reduced to stealing food and even licking greasy newspapers used to wrap food.

The author says nothing is more miserable than being an Irish catholic in poverty. But then, a happy childhood is hardly worth your while.

The book deals with his constant inner conflicts, health issues, and series of church confessions and ends when he leaves for the USA to seek a better future. Ironically, he uses part of the stolen money—the rest comes from his savings from years of odd jobs, starting in his early teens.

There is nothing more moving than seeing the poor, hungry and helpless. And nothing tells failure of society and its chief organ of transformation - administration - than to read about a profoundly unequal society, where some live in obscene opulence while others live on the margin - statistical callisthenics notwithstanding.

It was all too easy for well-fed Indians in Singapore to shout in Unison that India was a great success story during Rahul Gandhi's recent visit. I wish I were there to scream at the top of my voice that No, No, No—India is not successful, as we still have thousands of Limericks and millions of Franks among us.

This is not a political issue. All governments have failed to bridge the gap and to provide the basic needs to all Indians. Schemes come and go, ditto for Governments. Poor remain where they were. We lack genuine compassion, intent, consistency in approach and single-minded focus.

Low-income people exist everywhere - their proportion, intensity and hope for amelioration change across society. India, sadly, is at the tragic end of it.

Communists in India had the best chance to represent people with low incomes. Still, they held on to the apron strings of an alien philosophy, imported role models and undemocratic models of governance and delivery. Unwisely, they also believed in the uniformity of outcomes rather than the uniformity of opportunities. No wonder they are fast becoming an anachronism. I wish they had metamorphosed into something like European Social Democrats, with Indigenous role models and a deep commitment to uplifting those left behind.

A karmic cycle is in waiting. Israeli historian Harari says that with the advent of artificial intelligence, more and more wealth will be concentrated in the hands of a few, and the rest of humanity will stare at joblessness across continents. Without wealth redistribution, the current rich and poor would be on the same side of the fence.

One wonders if the future gives hope to Frank McCourts or if thousands of Limericks are waiting to mushroom all around us.

60

Modi Bashing

Then, the borders were calm;
Highways lined with lovely palm;
Benevolent govt. applied soothing balm;
Lakes were clean where swan swam;
No corruption, no one heard of scam;
In came Modi with his ugly plan.

Then, all around prevailed peace;
Everyone's plate had bread and cheese;
The weather was consistently cool, with a gentle breeze;
All were healthy, not even a sneeze;
Politicians had character, no one heard of sleaze;
Secular were even the ISIS;
In came Modi with his venomous hiss.

Then, every Indian had a job;
One could walk miles and not find a snob;
Govt. largesse available on turning a knob;
There were no cow vigilante mad mob;
Everyone was happy, and one never heard one sob;
In came Modi, turned nation into a burning hob.

Then, every Indian beamed a feel-good smile;

Content within, you could spot from a mile;
Bonhomie lingered on for a while;
Ah, so soothing was to watch a married couple walk the aisle in style;
The nation prospered through providential design;
In came Modi, you ugly and vile.

Then, every home had power;
Everyone had running water and a shower;
Life was calm, content were the lovers;
One could relax for hours under the garden bower;
Communal relations never turned sour;
In came Modi and made everyone tremor.

Then, no dynasty reigned pure merit;
Good deeds abound, accorded due credit;
Everything available in plenty, no need to ferret;
Govt. spending remained within limit;
Press and social media were free, without censorship or edit;
In came Modi, the stupid.

Oh, where did the halcyon days go?
Why did we get, Modi, the Shrew?
    [P.S. - This is a work of satire and should be read as such.]

EARTH & ENVIRONMENT

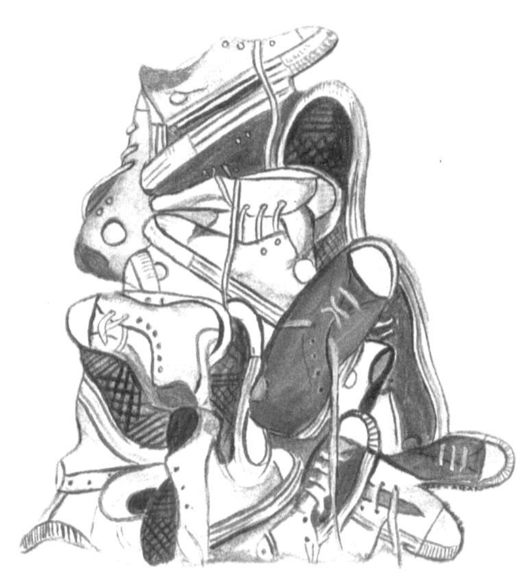

61

The Great Arc

Any sufficiently advanced technology is indistinguishable from magic.
- Arthur C. Clarke

Did you know that Sir George Everest (pronounced as 'Eve'rest, as in Adam and Eve) was not a mountaineer, or for that matter, possibly never saw the highest peak in the world? Instead, he was the first surveyor general of India from 1830 onwards, and along with his illustrious predecessor, William Lambton, he was involved in something profound from a scientific perspective and for surveying British India as it was expanding its tentacles across the length and breadth of India.

I did not know these until I read this excellent book, *'The Great Arc'*, by Scottish Journalist John Keay. The author masterfully takes you on a journey back to the early nineteenth century, when the tremendous trigonometric survey of India was undertaken and alternates with travel within contemporary India.

The exact shape of the earth was a puzzle, and attempts were made to measure it precisely by measuring the ark along longitude in Britain. However, they did not have the required length of the arc for precise measurement. The expanding British Raj afforded this opportunity. To the East India Company, this served an additional purpose of surveying and consolidating the hold over their occupied territory from a revenue perspective.

This survey was one of the most exciting scientific and geographic research undertaken at the time, covered extensively by the Royal Geographic Survey and other publications. The total cost was estimated at Pound 150,000 and started in the early eighteen hundred and beyond the First War of Independence in 1957. Interestingly, in some measure, it also fueled discontent among natives and contributed, in a small way, to the Great War.

With the prevailing technology and the wilderness of good parts of India (jungles, tigers, mosquitoes), it was a challenging task, and it was left to Lambton to commence precise measurement, starting from Madras. Their equipment was a 100-meter precise chain (later on compensating iron and brass bars), another custom-made one to keep calibrating in a controlled environment, and a heavy theodolite. Any repair had to be done in the UK itself.

The method adopted was to use a triangle (usually 6 miles on each side, but gradually increased to 60 and more), place measurement scales atop high grounds such as hills, temple tops, etc. and measure the angles (horizontal and vertical) using the theodolite. And, of course, complex mathematical equations (30 odd) to arrive at results. Any error, such as human error, refraction, chain expansion due to heat and wear & tear, etc., had a compounding effect, and hence, multiple measurements from each side were carried out. And frequent modifications of hand-scribbled mathematical formulae were needed.

Once a triangle was completed, a new triangle was formed, using one side as the base. The team kept expanding to other sides—Bangalore, Mysore, Hyderabad, and Malabar. Counter measurements with heavenly objects were carried out to ensure reliability.

Monsoon and post-monsoon were considered best to ensure better visibility, but they were also the most inconvenient (flooded rivers, heavy jungle undergrowth, mosquitoes, and hungry tigers). Over time, they graduated to oil lamps at the end of the scale (and early morning measurement, when refraction error was minimal) and then to chemical flares.

The book offers a fascinating account of the challenges faced and how the indomitable spirit of surveyors, foot soldiers and the lateral thinking of leadership was used to overcome them. For example, the great Indian plane offered very few elevated areas, and new watch towers had to be created. Or, even after several careful measurements, when they could not reconcile, they discovered that the plumb line deviates from vertical in the presence of mountains and cavities on Earth! Formulae needed correction.

It also gives an insightful account of personalities and their work ethics. Lambton was an Indian admirer, affable, and trusted his people, and once, while transporting the theodolite to the top of Brihadeswara temple, it slipped and was damaged. Lambton got it repaired at his own cost at Rupee 8 million at the current price. On the other hand, Everest was boorish, choleric and ever-carping. He was prone to frequent illness and needed breaks. He had no regrets about riding roughshods, for example, razing down houses and trees if they came in the line of the site for measurement.

It offers some interesting tidbits, such as British surveyors taking their family and entire retinue, tents, etc., on elephant and horseback and expanding their families in hostile geographies!

Everest settled in Mussoorie because it offered a good view of the mountains and a salubrious climate. He was instrumental in setting up the survey of India at Dehradun. The city still proudly retains the chains and other artefacts of the era.

They also faced challenges from the Orthodox. How else would the natives see if someone is observing through an eyeglass in the early morning, showing all (especially women) inverted? Or, for that matter, burn fires and flares on hilltops and mark territories through stones. Shamanic work?

How did this lead to Mount Everest's measurement? Well. The British had no access to the mountains, as Nepal was hostile. Only the redoubtable Sir William Jones and a few more had hazarded the Himalayan mountains to be the highest in the world, with varying guestimates. Only when the survey gradually reached the edge of British India, conquered Garhwal and Kumaon, and got a breathtaking view of the entire Himalayan range could they measure the mountains with any certainty. And on maps, they were named X, P, K, etc. (K2 retains the name)

By then, Everest had retired, and his successor recommended his name for the highest peak.

The book spares tortuous mathematical equations and can be safely enjoyed by those who fear quadratic equations.

62

Save Humanity

You don't live on earth, you are passing through.
- Rumi

I was watching a video clip and imagining (rather, building up a scenario) what would happen if all human beings were to disappear tomorrow morning.

Essentially, it predicted that all power plants would shut down in a few hours, plunging the earth into darkness. Underground metros would be flooded. Nuclear power plants will erupt (in the absence of controls and heavy water), plunging the planet into radiological toxicity. Most animals may die, and those who survive will become wild predators. Artefacts created by humans will gradually crumble over a few hundred years, deserts and water bodies shall overtake, and cities will be consumed by nature (forests, deserts, etc.).

On the positive side, the air will be cleaner, and visibility will improve. Over tens of thousands of years, nature will return to its pre-human stage, and possibly, new organisms will take over the Earth.

Mind you, the scenario does not predict planet Earth's disappearance.

That brings me to another interesting take by comedian Late George Carlin. Carlin says it is arrogant for humans to talk about saving other creatures or even the Earth. Remember the *'Save the Planet'* campaign?

He reasons, in his style, that the Earth has been around for several billion years (4.5 billion years, as estimated by scientists) and has witnessed many violent cataclysms, worse than what we are perpetrating - lack of air, earthquakes, volcanic eruptions, bolts of lightning, toxic showers, floodings (pluvial age) prolonged winters (ice age), asteroids, collision with other heavenly objects (resulting in the creation of moon). But it has survived. Humans have been around for a million years or less (widely believed that genre Homo started with Homo Erectus - bipedal creatures, around 1.6 million years back), and the entire industrial revolution is less than two hundred years. It is presumptuous to think that we have created plastic and, hence, are choking the Earth to death and therefore, we need to save the world, humans and other creatures.

Mother Earth is far more significant and older than the human race. It has also seen the growth, extinction, and obliteration of far more successful creatures - Dinosaurs roamed around and ruled the earth for over 180 million years. Yet, we can see their fossil in museums only now. And if you think the Earth worries about global warming, think again. If half of the land is inundated with the melting snow of the polar caps, humans have less space to live - the Earth couldn't care. These are all her children.

So, my take is that rather than celebrating '*Save Earth Day,*' we should celebrate and create awareness through '*Save Human Race*' day.

The Earth is going nowhere, but our actions will precipitate our extinction from the universe. Mother Earth will not lose one minute of sleep over our exit. Possibly, she will not even notice it. We are far too insignificant.

If we want to prolong our stay (mind you, I am not talking about immortality or staying forever—we shall be extinct one day, which is how nature works), we should look for alternative abodes—other planets, as recommended by Physicist Stephen Hawking.

Till then, it makes sense for us to live in harmony. It is better for Kim Jong Un and Trump to collaborate to use their nuclear arsenal to destroy incoming asteroids than accelerate our collective annihilation.

175

63

Water Management

If there is magic on this planet, it is contained in water.
- Loren Eiseley

So, the rains are around the corner. Fields look verdant, and you can taste moisture in the air. Very soon, reservoirs will be full. But how long? A few months from now, we will witness familiar scenes of water scarcity.

India gets a reasonable amount of precipitation. So, why do we have water shortages?

This is because we lack 'Water Management.' So, let's explore the components of water management.

1) *Supply* - Discounting micro sources such as cloud seeding and reverse osmosis, the sole source of water is rain. Rain depends on many factors, including green cover and, as a long-term trend, global warming. As against the recommended 33% green forests, we have around 20%, which is depleting. Globally, we plant one tree for every four we chop down. Unless we undertake afforestation on a large scale, nationally and internationally, especially in catchment areas, hills and the countryside, we are looking down the barrel.

2) *Storage* - Open reservoirs are a very inefficient way of storage due to high evaporation and seepage. Experiments have been successfully done on storage in naturally found underground crevices between rock layers, for example, in Australia. Plastic balls have been left afloat in the USA, covering entire lakes to reduce

evaporation loss. A simple and successful way of storage in India has been through check dams. By creating barriers to the easy flow of rainwater, we force it to percolate down, thereby increasing the water table. As a tropical nation, I suspect we lose much more through evaporation than other nations.

3) *Transportation* - Ideally, there should be little need for transportation, especially over long distances. Water pipes from relatively arid central Maharashtra to Mumbai are a shame. Mumbai gets much more rain than the rest of the state. Open canals from significant rivers are not only open to evaporation and seepage loss but also contribute to the pollution of rivers (due to lack of water downstream) and alter the crop pattern in faraway places. In any case, water transport should be through underground aqueducts. Learn from ancient Middle Eastern and Indian civilisations.

4) *Consumption* - Optimal consumption means minimising wastage. While households must take every step to reduce waste, enormous industrial and agricultural waste contributes much more. It makes no sense for arid regions in Maharashtra, UP, and Rajasthan to grow rice and cane sugar. Buy these from nations better equipped to produce them. More often than not, the rich and powerful corner the Lion's share of available water. Price water properly for Industries to incentivise them to optimise.

5) *Recycle*—The nation needs to recycle water as much as possible. Rainwater, kitchen water, and Industrial water can be locally recycled to reduce dependency on transported water.

They say water is life. Do we treat it like our breath? What if we run out of it one awful day?

64

Prevent Wastage

The greatest threat to our planet is the belief that someone else will save it.

- Robert Swan

The other day, I stopped at a '*Cafe Coffee Day*' to grab a quick cup of coffee. I observed that the unused sugar pouches were discarded in the waste bin even though they were clean. The same evening, I visited a decent restaurant and observed wastage in terms of portions of food and beverages.

Just reflect on how much we waste, mostly unconsciously. I want to draw your attention to the waste we cause around us.

We waste water while brushing our teeth, shaving, bathing, washing vessels, and using water filters. Little care can reduce, reuse and recycle a significant part of it.

If you find the portion at a restaurant too large, please feel free to return it before eating. Of course, restaurants should analyse the situation and consider offering a smaller portion at a lower price.

We should inculcate in our children the importance of not wasting food on their plates, even at home. Do not cook more than you consume. Eating a little less is healthier than overconsumption.

Hotels are big wasters of resources. Soaps, shampoo, linen...Do you know that many high-end European hotels now offer liquid soap in a dispenser? And linens are not replaced daily if you stay longer than a day.

Our inefficient supply chain management and lack of a cold chain have led to a colossal waste of food grains, vegetables, and fruits. This waste also robs the growers of the fair value of their labour and puts additional pressure on Mother Earth.

One can go on and on. I would be happy to get your views on other examples of waste around you and how we can reduce it.

Just reflect. If we waste 10% of global resources, we deprive 800 million people worldwide of their rights to resources. This is well over half of India's population and is larger than the people living on the margins of society in large parts of the world.

Can we do our bit to reduce wastage? While the institutions take their time to set things right and curb wastage?

65
Return Chain Management

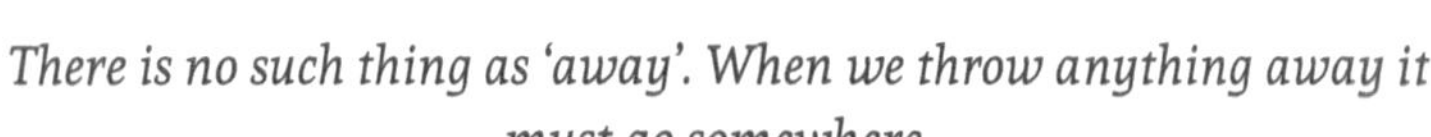

There is no such thing as 'away'. When we throw anything away it must go somewhere.
- Annie Leonard

What will you see if you visit the nearest mom-and-pop store to pick up a loaf of bread?

'Best use by' date. Right?

If this date is today, you may not take it.

You may even let the shop owner know if it was yesterday.

What about expired medicines? What nonsense. Indeed, you will not touch an expired medicine.

But this is precisely what the US military does. Given their size, they buy a lot of just-expired medicines at a fraction of the cost and consume them quickly.

Why?

Because the medicines do not become poison the day after their expiry date, they gradually lose their potency. Of course, it is necessary to store it hygienically.

This is true for most items with an expiry date. Some become stale in a few days, but medicines have a much longer half-life.

Yet, at your neighbourhood store, kilos of 'stale' expired food items are discarded daily—Ditto at the medical shop.

Manufacturers will tell you that much of the produce is returned as they return unsold.

Could we extend the logic further? Vegetable shops, restaurants, milk, curd, and groceries are everywhere. We have robust supply chain management (yes, robust, because you always get it). But, we lack 'Return Chain Management'. Call it RCM.

By RCM, I mean returning stuff just before its expiry date while it remains functional, safe, and hygienic. I also mean returning it optimally to reach those in need who cannot afford to buy it.

In a country where millions of poor people cannot afford food, medicines, milk, or vegetables, we need to consider RCM to reduce waste and provide for those who need it.

It costs very little to organise it, and it is environmentally friendly, too. After all, all manufacturing consumes part of the earth's produce and the sun's energy. Right?

66

Plastic Menace

If it can't be reduced, reused, repaired, rebuilt, refurbished, refinished, resold, recycled, or composted, then it should be restricted, designed or removed from production.
- Pete Seeger

In the good old days of my childhood, we were far wiser and environmentally sensitive.

Most shops dispensed with provisions in paper bags (brown ones at bigger shops, ones made of newspaper and used copybooks at local shops). The shop fellow packed our provisions in gunny bags, and for liquids, such as oil, we would carry our bottles or jars. Old clothes were recycled into grocery bags before finding 'Nirvana' as dusters and floor mops.

Even milk was delivered in glass bottles—we would surrender the previous day's milk to get fresh milk in a new bottle.

Instead of using dishwashing liquid, it was common to use ash, and in many homes, natural stuff like reetha was used to wash clothes. It was common to use besan as soap and shikakai to wash hair. Then we had coconut fibre in place of plastic mesh to scrub vessels, burnt brick to scrub iron panes (*tava*) in place of iron filing, tamarind to clean brassware instead of chemical polish, turmeric water to clean floors, marigold leaf juice as a disinfectant...The list can go on...

No, not for a moment, I am alluding that we were chemical-free, but alternatives were used as often.

Today, even at some organic food shops, provisions are packed in non-biodegradable plastics. Small to large shops have discovered the ease of pre-packing stuff in plastic pouches and bags.

If you look around, two distinct plastic items contribute to most of the plastic you see around - plastic water bottles (an eyesore wherever you go) and plastic bags. And what we try to tackle are sippers and plastic stirrers!

No one is serious about a plastic ban, as evidenced by the fact that no plastic bag manufacturer has been forced to close down, and no serious attempt has been made to provide alternative ways of dispensing clean drinking water.

If you observe closely, tourism (including hotels and travel) and airlines are the most significant plastics users. And an abominable amount of waste, too. Could you observe how much shampoo and soap you waste during your hotel stay?

It is good that efforts are underway to create awareness and find alternatives. But are we not too late already? Plastic islands are larger than many islands in the ocean and are expected to overtake entire fish populations. Plastic and chemicals are entering our system through animal and plant products. And you can hear more about cancer and other dreaded diseases than ever before.

Not all plastic is bad. Long-lasting stuff like furniture, bathroom doors, and even rain covers are desirable, as they serve the purpose inexpensively and can be the end product for plastic bags and PET bottles, which currently end up in ponds, rivers, and oceans. I don't know about storage jars and bottles, as these are not good for food products.

Ironically, we are far better educated and have more access to information than ever. But our ancestors had access to better wisdom - maybe from a higher source. They were in greater synergy with Earth and nature.

Otherwise, why would they have written in Yajurveda

ॐ द्यौः शान्तिरन्तरिक्षँ शान्तिः,
पृथ्वी शान्तिराप: शान्तिरोषधय: शान्ति:।
वनस्पतय: शान्तिर्विश्वे देवा: शान्तिर्ब्रह्म शान्ति:,
सर्वं शान्ति:, शान्तिरेव शान्ति:, सा मा शान्तिरेधि॥
ॐ शान्ति: शान्ति: शान्ति:॥

Om dyauḥ śāntirantarikṣaṁ śāntiḥ,
pṛthvī śāntirāpaḥ śāntiḥ roṣadhayaḥ śāntiḥ.
vanaspatayḥ śāntirviśve devāḥ śāntirbrahma śāntiḥ,
sarvaṁ śāntiḥ, śāntireva śāntiḥ, sā mā śāntiredhi.
Om śāntiḥ śāntiḥ śāntiḥ.
[Om, peace be in the heavens, peace in the sky,
peace on Earth, peace in the waters, peace in the plants and herbs.
Peace in the trees, peace in all the gods, peace in the supreme Brahman,
peace in all, peace alone, may that peace come to me.
Om, peace, peace, peace.

67

Banning Use of Plastic

It cannot be right to manufacture billions of objects that are used for a matter of minutes, and then are with us for centuries.

- Roz Savage

The current rules relating to the ban on plastic carry bags are inadequate and have been implemented half-heartedly; therefore, they have not made any difference in environmental degradation due to the ever-increasing use of plastic.

We all know about the impact of plastic use on our environment, landfills, urban squalor, farm produce, animal and even marine life. Finally, it finds its way into our bodies through the ingestion of microplastics, leading to enormous health complications, including cancer.

There is enough scientific research to prove the deleterious effect of plastic on human and animal life, indeed on our mother planet.

Plastic is non-biodegradable and will remain on our planet for over five hundred years, even if we stop producing it. The sad part is that more and more plastic is being made even as we speak.

The reason for the increased use of plastic is not difficult to see. It provides enormous convenience in packing and transportation, is inexpensive to produce and dispense with, and the producer does not need to worry about return and recycling. Unfortunately, that job is left to those at the bottom of our socioeconomic life - the rag pickers and scavengers.

It is even more regrettable that alternatives now exist in reusable packaging, biodegradable material, etc. Not so long ago, it was common to see milk in glass bottles or people carrying jute bags to shops, as plastic carry bags had not even been invented.

Stronger laws, sincere enforcement, deterrent punishments, and higher costs associated with using plastic, in whatever form, are needed.

I therefore request the Indian Central government to take the initiative and pass laws along the following lines.

1) A time-bound ban on importing and producing plastic material, except for durables. The manufacturing units need to switch to biodegradable alternatives. Unless the manufacture of plastic is stopped, it will continue to find its way into our homes.

2) Financial incentives and rewards for research and development to find viable alternatives to plastic. Government laboratories should lead in this direction and collaborate with private efforts. The fruits of such research should be made available to manufacturers of plastic produce, free of any royalty or charges.

3) A time-bound action plan to force producers and suppliers to switch to biodegradable alternatives and reusable packaging. This should apply uniformly to manufacturers of consumer goods, groceries, milk, wafers, courier supplies, imports, etc. The list is endless, such is the stranglehold of plastic in our lives.

4) Until alternatives are found, make it mandatory for producers and suppliers to arrange to pick up plastic waste generated through their supplies. They must mandatorily set up 'reverse supply chain management' to pick up the plastic from the point of sale and dispose of it scientifically - the cost of setting up this infrastructure to be built into the price of produce. Consumers need to be aware of the cost of environmental degradation and raise their voices for biodegradable alternatives, at least to bring down the end price of their consumption. Do read the second segment for a possible approach.

5) To incentivise consumers to participate in zero plastic waste efforts, a high cost must be associated with plastic packaging, which

could be a deposit. In return for packing at the point of sale, the consumer may be refunded the deposit or can adjust against future purchases. The high deposit cost will encourage consumers to be willing partners in recycling and scientific waste management.

6) Finally, to recognise the valuable service rag pickers provide, the government must train them in the scientific collection, provide them with safety gear, incentivise them through adequate compensation and medical benefits, protect them from drug abuse, and reward them with old-age pensions.

You would agree that plastic goods' convenience and low price are illusory, as our children will pay the actual cost of suffocating the earth, having a poorer quality of life, and, finally, reaching a point of no return.

II

a) The Government should make bar code (or QR code) mandatory for every plastic item. The bar code should include colour, plastic-type, container type (bottle, jerrycan, wrapper, etc.), usage (toxic, oil, milk, dry eatables, etc.), and price. It should be mandatory for all to use a bar-coded plastic bag for packing and dispensing.

b) When buying anything, one should also pay for the packaging, which will be reflected separately in the invoice. This will be a considerable amount, and the cost incurred for plastic should be shown in the invoice.

c) One can return the plastic to a designated collection centre, where one can get a full refund. The bar code will help the collection centre process it quickly. One can do this every week or month whenever you're free. All refunds can be done using digital means.

d) The collection centre shall segregate them based on barcode and send them to the processing centre, where they will be segregated for reuse, recycled into plastic durables, or used in road construction. Canny shopkeepers shall set up a collection centre at their shop itself to win customer loyalty by providing convenience.

e) If one does not return plastic for recycling and discard it because one thinks one's time is more precious than the considerable amount one has paid for the wrapper, one need not worry. The rag picker will do it for one and get much higher compensation at collection centres. One will help create a market.

f) All those industries that create plastic should be made to contribute to setting up the processing centre.

g) This model can be extended beyond plastic to glass bottles, medicine bottles, metal strips for medicines, hard card packaging, metal cans, tetra packs, flax banners and plywood packaging. Everything other than the content should be priced adequately and incentivised to return, and a return supply chain management should be set up.

h) Of course, there would be a margin at every step - for collection and processing centres - all of which should be built into what the end consumer pays. This may attract many entrepreneurs and startups to set up city and township centres.

Do you think this is farfetched? Go to Germany, and you will see people faithfully returning used glass bottles at the supermarket and collecting refunds. And they are far more prosperous than we are.

If Germans can do it and segregate waste, why not us?

And why should the polluters not pay? Are they producers, suppliers, or consumers like you and I?

68
End of Earth

Endings are scary and foreign. They split you up emotionally and put you in a place where you don't know what's going to happen next. But with every end of the world, there is a new world that follows.
- Alex Hirsch

Celebrated Physicist Stephen Hawking warned that we have a limited time window available before we must leave Mother Earth. He had given Homo Sapiens as little as a century to move away. Just a century to find new habitats, develop new eating habits, make new daily routines and create new avocations to keep us busy and procreate.

Many things could go wrong on earth. Climactic changes, epidemics, atomic war, overpopulation...then things happening inside the planet - volcanoes, earthquakes. Or, some astral object colliding with earth. There are millions of these around us. And, if you believe science fiction author Asimov, there could be an alien invasion.

Earth is known to have witnessed violent events. Remember the decimation of Dinosaurs, who ruled Earth for millions of years? In comparison, bipedalism (of our distant ancestors, Homo Erectus) is less than a million years old; Homo Sapiens arrived at the scene less than 50,000 years back after painful, often violent and serendipitous Darwinian selection.

To us, Homo Sapiens, it is a painful thought that we are neither Lords of all things - big or small - nor infinite on the temporal scale and, indeed, not invincible or indestructible.

It should be a humbling thought. All that we witness around us or artefacts we have created - technology right up to quantum computers, automation, the age of the machines, cinema, impressive knowledge, convenience, conquering space, and clairvoyance - have all been acquired over the last century or two. Fine arts and literature are relatively old, and so is religion. But, all these are, together, less than a couple of steps if you consider solidifying gaseous elements into the earth as the beginning of one marathon race.

So, how will it feel to leave Earth? Imagine sitting in an imaginary spaceship on our last journey from Earth with a single-way ticket. Imagine our blue, cloud-covered planet, consisting of three-fourths water, receding in the background - from a large ball to a small one, then a dot disappearing into the horizon.

How humbling or reflective could that last journey be?

That down below, we fought internecine battles over land, proved our racial superiority, asserted our anthropocentric superiority over weaker creatures, obliterated flora and fauna for our consumption, and asserted gender and political supremacy.

Of leaving behind art and literature, God (and fighting over our God vs yours), scriptures, colours, artefacts, and conveniences. Of our socio-political accomplishments and endless debates, of minerals and metals, of endless conveniences. Of a lifestyle. Of our heritage and remains of near and dear ones. One day, it will all just disappear into the giant Universe.

Would we carry our angst and remorse, or would faith be the only thing to provide us with solace? Or literature? Would we hope that our children pick up at least part of what we accomplished?

While we are still away from our imaginary spaceship on our last journey, is it not better that we continue to be better human beings today? Of not beheading fellow human beings in the name of religion and land?

Did our ancestors have prescience about it when they advocated peaceful coexistence and submission to the higher power?

And, will we only remember Nawab Wajid Ali Khan on his last journey from Lucknow to Kolkata, having lost his principality to the British, and shall hum.

"Babul mora, Naihar chuta jay"

[O my father, my maternal home is being left behind]

FAITH & RELIGION

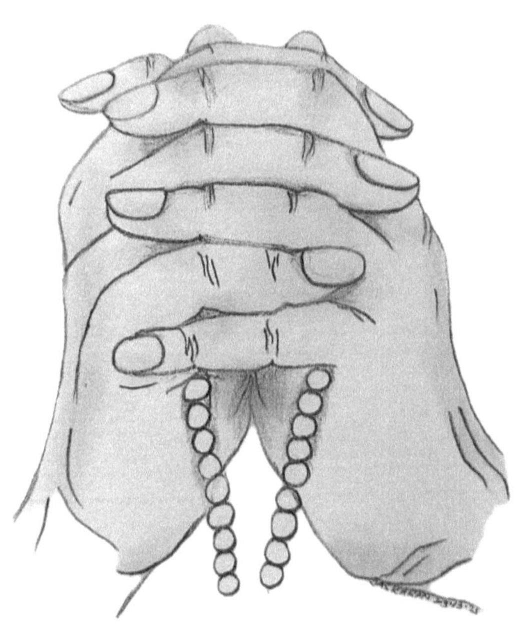

69

Faith, Religion and Science

Faith is the bird that feels the light when the dawn is still dark.
- Rabindranath Tagore

I watched a brilliant dialogue between celebrated author Devdutt Pattnaik and N. Ram of '*The Hindu*' about faith, religion, and science.

Faith is people's beliefs, and our entire lives are based on faith and assumptions—like our parentage, our banking system, and money itself, which is nothing more than faith in its exchangeability.

Concepts like money are called 'intersubjective' beliefs. They may not be objective facts in the real sense, but many people widely believe them to be correct and, hence, work.

When nothing is going right, faith holds us, gives us patience, and illuminates our way forward.

Faith is not to be tested based on logic or rational thinking. They are of different dimensions.

I was watching an interview with a doctor who talks about a patient suffering from some brain disease, living entirely upon faith in the doctor's words and hope. The moment the doctor gave up hope, the patient died.

The author says science is presented as a modern-day religion. It is not. Science deals with facts, measurements, and evidence. Truth, on the other hand, is the domain of religion.

To add, a century ago, science considered the atom indivisible. This was the truth then, but later experiments proved otherwise. Truth is unchangeable, but evidence and measurements yield new facets and dimensions.

In the realm of truth, we have a continuum from fantasy (which no one believes) to myth (which is someone's personal belief system) to truth (which is everyone's belief system).

If someone believes in a myth but is not harming anyone else or challenging any contemporary understanding, there is no harm in letting them hold it. It provides fuzziness and allows for conversation and negotiations.

For example, suppose someone believes that Ganesh's head was a successful transplant and ancient Indians had aeroplanes. In that case, it does not harm anyone unless we refuse to move forward, stop all technological progress, and start living entirely in past glory.

Problems arise when someone's myth is judged upon, scoffed at, and eager to be proved wrong. Such a binary judgment, as against the continuum, creates friction and intolerance.

And this is precisely what we are witnessing. Rather than being patient with individual faith, respecting belief in personal God and myths, and allowing space for hope even in the face of hopelessness, the liberal, rational, and educated are far too obsessed with proving others wrong.

Alas, the world is not binary, but computer programs are. Mercifully, the world has more human tissues and neurons than electronic bits and bytes.

70

Why I am a Hindu

India is the meeting place of the religions and among these Hinduism alone is by itself a vast and complex thing, not so much a religion as a great diversified and yet subtly unified mass of spiritual thought, realization and aspiration.

- Sri Aurobindo

'Why I am a Hindu' is Sashi Tharoor's latest religio-political book, and he has lived up to the expectations of being an erudite political scholar.

The first part, consisting of about 100 pages, traces the journey of Hinduism from the days of the Vedas, the Shruti and Smriti traditions, Upanishads, Itihas, Puranas, and Darshans.

It emphasises the all-inclusive, liberal, eclectic (a word he often uses in the book) and ever-evolving nature of Hinduism. He emphasises that Hinduism never claims to be 'revealed', has no single authoritative and binding text for its believers, and accepts that there is one truth which can be reached through multiple routes. The author traces Hinduism's evolution over the ages and how it faced challenges - first within the religion by those who had different viewpoints (for example, Patanjali with his disciplined Ashtanga Yoga and Charvaka with his epicureanism), and thereafter by religious movements which originated within India viz. Buddhism and Jainism.

And how, through its internal dynamics and willingness to accommodate and evolve, the religion took different aspects from other religious movements.

Tharoor also covers the Advaitha by Adi Shankara and his outstanding contribution to the Hindu Renaissance, Dwaita by Ramanujam and similar bhakti movements by various saints such as Kabir, Tualsidas, Madhavacharya, etc., to make religion easy to follow and observe by the masses.

The author touches upon the onslaught of Islamists and Christians, the hardship faced by Hindus and how they could survive; in fact, they even made the conquerors focus on territorial and political domination, leaving Hindus essentially alone in their religious practices.

In modern times, the author discusses Vivekananda, Rammohun Roy, Dayanand, Narayan Guru, and Gandhi and how they advanced religion through introspection, observations, and interpretation while remaining rooted in the social milieu.

The first part is commendable in its profundity, simplicity, and logic and can enrich the knowledge of even keen and well-read students of Hinduism.

The second part is more political and justifiably reflects Tharoor's political leanings. It starts with the narrow and dogmatic view of religion as perceived by the Hindu Mahasabha and the cultural, geographic, and even racial views of RSS, which evolved into Jana Sangh and later BJP.

The author quotes from the writings of Savarkar, Hegdewar, Golvalkar, and then Deen Dayal Upadhyaya. He does not miss a chance to take potshots at Savarkar for seeking clemency from the British during his incarceration at Cellular Jail, Andaman Islands.

Tharoor talks about the near proselytising religious approach of these right-wingers, how they were closer to the Nazi approach of the superiority of their identity and promoted a subsidiary role for the minorities unless they accepted their unison with the dominating culture of India.

He has praise for the *'Integral Humanism'* of Deen Dayal Upadhyaya (which, funnily, rhymes well with the 'Radical Humanism' of MN Roy, a staunch communist and the opposite left end of the spectrum). Still, he is sceptical of Deen Dayal Upadhyaya and Balraj Madhok. In his typical, condescending attitude, the author avers that they could afford to appear inclusive and accommodative to minorities, as they had not hoped to be ever able to come to power.

He has reserved his harshest criticism for the current government and has quoted various incidents to portray the ruling dispensation as narrow, lacking in intellectual depth, regressive, and capable of having a deleterious effect on not only the body politic and the social fabric of the nation but also the religion itself.

Interestingly, the author does not see any harm in Christian missionaries trying to convert Hindus. He believes those against conversion should provide counterinducments of a similar or higher nature. He trusts that Hindus who trust its inherent eclectic strength shall remain Hindus. I don't know if this is the case.

Tharoor also questions the lack of right-wingers' involvement in the freedom struggle. I want to discuss this with him.

Firstly, the freedom struggle was not only a congress movement, even though history books written by congress-supported historians would like us to believe so. Many different opinions and approaches existed during the freedom struggle, and not all aligned with Congress, yet they contributed to freedom at midnight.

Secondly, by denying legitimacy to the BJP because it is not involved in the freedom struggle, the author seems to justify the Congress' perpetual rule as if it were a 'right' - a kind of perpetual dividend.

Congress cannot claim this right by dint of its name, just like India cannot lay claim on everything in this land and deny Pakistan its due share of our collective history.

Finally, Congress' history is more than just the history of a single-family lineage. I'm unsure if Congress greats will recognise the present-day Congress as theirs if they come back to life from their graves for once.

Tharoor may be smug in Congress lineage. To me, it looks hoary.

71

Ills of Hinduism

Arise, awake, and stop not until the goal is achieved.
- Swami Vivekananda

It is easy to converse on anodyne topics, but we must sometimes reflect on our religious belief system and practices. It is not that Muslim personal law has all the ills or that Hindu practices are perfect. No one is. Every belief must be re-examined and course-corrected if not aligned with contemporary values.

The biggest strength of Hinduism has been its ability to evolve and purge itself at critical times. Reformers have not been shunned but, more often, welcomed.

For example, it is well known that high caste Hindus were meat eaters (I do not believe in the beef eating theory, though. Pastoral would not eat beef. The Rig Vedic hymn, which is often quoted, is a Sanskrit translation. Vedas were not written in Sanskrit!). However, under the influence of Jainism, when kings and subjects started embracing their value system, especially non-violence, Hindu society evolved. We rediscovered ourselves, brick by brick. Remember Adi Shankaracharya. Remember the pantheons written on temple walls?

More recently, Ram Mohan Roy and many others worked on several social ills and attempted to purge Hindu society. Bengali *Kulin* system (young girls being married off to old males of high caste), *Sati* system (women dying with husband on a funeral pyre) or child marriage have been primarily contained. Exceptions remain, though.

However, a few Hindu practices trouble me, and I will not shy away from writing about them. My limited reading of scriptures, especially Vedas, Upanishads and Bhagavad Gita, indicate that these practices do not originate in the grand tradition. They owe their genesis to the Puranas, such as Garud Purana and Manu smriti, the middle-aged text. Puranas were stories, often containing contradictory values and outlandish claims. Many of our social ills have their root in these little traditions, and Hindu scholars and religious leaders have done a great disservice by not denouncing these half-baked works of inferior minds.

That the caste system is pernicious, inhuman, and divisive and keeps a section of society away from social contribution, social mobility and reaping the benefits is well understood. An extreme form has been untouchability. Let us accept that it does exist, even today. Dining together is standard, but exceptions exist, especially in a traditional milieu. Every time I go to any famous temple and am invited to partake in lunch exclusively, due to my caste, I feel very odd and guilty.

Society has yet to treat widows as equals, though progressive forces have made widow remarriage easier. And I am not referring to thousands of widows at Vrindavan but to those who are part of our family. Do we treat them equally, especially on auspicious occasions, religious rituals, and gift-giving? In most families, they are not.

What about the distribution of wealth? Almost all succession happens along male lines. What girls get in a lavish marriage (which is often wasteful) is *dowry* (outlawed) or gifts. Indeed, this is not a fair division of wealth. And because dowry (*Stree dhan*) is undocumented and unregistered, it is challenging for a girl to take it with her should the marriage fail.

What I find most detesting is the ritual around the death ceremony. At a time when the family is most vulnerable (emotionally, energy-wise and also financially, having spent a fortune on treatment) and needs maximum emotional support, society reduces its interaction. Remember the limited social visits? Bath after visiting? Also, the 13-day rituals, rice balls, feeding the crows, ritual bath, treatment of the recently widowed, the never-ending donations to make the afterlife of departed soul comfortable...They are mean, expensive and emotionally sapping. Incidentally, these elaborate rituals were never part of great tradition, even though Hinduism has always been soul-centric rather than God-centric.

I think, as a progressive religion, Hinduism should reflect on and find solutions to these ills.

72
National Anthem

<hr>

I feel unabashedly Indian, and this means that not just do I jump to my feet and sing along with the national anthem, it also makes me inexplicably sentimental, proud and teary-eyed.
- Barkha Dutt

I took umbrage when BBC and CNN kept referring to the partition as the separation of the Muslim majority Pakistan and the Hindooo (that is how they pronounce it) majority India in the context of our respective Independence days.

I would have preferred if they had kept religion out or at least credited our founding fathers with creating a secular nation despite the tumult. Or, the BBC should start calling itself the British (Christian, protestant dominated) Broadcasting Corporation.

(As an aside, most British do not visit churches except for marriage or funeral services.)

As a kid, well into the third and fourth decade after independence, I became aware of my linguistic and caste affiliations, much before my religious denomination. Because it did not matter. India lived as one nation till the British decided to create and exploit the wedge of religious identity and insecurity.

The Muslims who came to India were essentially plunderers or empire builders, not religious crusaders. If they were otherwise, they did a pretty lousy job and failed to convert most of us. Except for a handful of Muslims who came from Central Asia or the Middle

East, most Muslims in India are us - they converted under conviction, coercion or consideration.

Partition was a bloody affair, as it was poorly managed, and the British should take a fair share of the blame. Anyway, there was no case history of such mass migration in such a short period from which one could learn beforehand.

Even after independence, the violence between communities was very infrequent and, in most cases, over local irreligious issues. The added communal colour was politically expedient and journalistically juicy. The total loss in sectarian violence till the mid-eighties was less than that perpetrated by skinheads, white supremacists and the KKK in the USA and between football fans in the UK. Maybe add IRA violence.

The inept leadership of a dynastic PM opened up the wounds. He pandered shamelessly to the obscurantist elements of both communities (the Shah Bano case, denying even a small alimony to an old divorced Muslim woman and Ram Janmabhumi lock opening to allow prayers at a disputed religious site) to survive politically. Well, he didn't survive, anyway.

The revivalists on both sides exploited the resultant wedge. Unfortunately, the growth of Wahabi beliefs (which were alien to subcontinental tolerance and co-existence), the lure of puritanical Islam, the romanticism of Middle Eastern riches and, finally, terrorism added fuel to the fire.

The Hindu orthodoxy and neo-fundamentalism are like the proverbial demon whose life is inside a caged parrot, secured far away. You need to kill the parrot first. The parrot is Islamic fundamentalism. And it is getting narrower and more obdurate.

I can understand not chanting '*Bharat Mata ki Jai*'. I accept your reservations about '*Vande Mataram*'. But, now some idiots are saying that the National Anthem is anathema to Muslims and that religion is above the nation. Come on.

No one would notice or care if you stood along with others and did not chant the National Anthem. A few million crackpots do not matter in a nation of 1.25 billion (most Muslims do sing the National anthem; I am only referring to the minuscule minority who are misguided). But why make it public, debate over it and defend it?

One may justifiably argue what is so significant about the National Anthem and why patriotism should be measured by sheer lung power and specific intonations. My brief answer is that nationhood is part of intersubjective realities—something that does not exist in the objective world but is believed in by the population. The National Anthem and such symbolism are part of imagined realities.

My two cents is that Muslims DO NOT need to change. They should stick to what their elders did two generations back. Just remain integrated in the Indian ethos, be an integral part of India, and contribute to and share the joy and sorrow of your motherland. Your locus lies here, not in some imagined land.

My other advice is to look for, create, and nurture community leaders not associated with mosques. Peace and prosperity come with a forward look, not by delving into and narrowly interpreting scriptures by self-serving religious leaders.

BBC is wrong. India and Pakistan were not partitioned into Hindu and Muslim-majority nations. India is converting into a Hindu majoritarianism. And that is the travesty.

73

Indian Muslim and Their Insecurity

Do good to others, and goodness will come back to you.
- Prophet Muhammad (peace be upon him)

Was Shehnai Maestro Ustad Bismillah Khan Saheb a true Muslim? On the face of it, he was a picture of a pious and simple life (*Deen dharma*) and a five-time *Namazi*. Some Indian *ulemas* would say he was not. He used to play music (prohibited), had a picture of the Hindu Goddess Saraswati at his home, and played devotional music.

Was Dr Abdul Kalam a devoted Muslim? No. He practised yoga and meditation and read The Bhagavad Gita.

You got it? The problem is that some orthodox *ulemas* have defined Islam so narrowly that most of the 20 crore Indian Muslims would fall outside their definition of faithful followers. The number of such revivalist thinkers is not more than a few million, including their zealous followers, but they hold sway over an entire community. They are the favourites at the TV studio, as they make controversial, ultra-narrow and incendiary statements and attract counter fireworks. Good for TRP. Right? Yet, they do not represent most of the Muslims - professionals, artisans, Govt servants, men in uniform, peasants, weavers. Most of these common Muslims are busy eking out their living and have other things to worry about.

They are on the margin of religion, just like most Hindus are.

Why are they silent? How come winds of change, which are blowing across many Muslim-majority nations (I am referring to social changes like marriage and divorce), are not reaching India? Why are the common Muslims reduced to being silent supporters of a minority of orthodox ulemas?

In my view, there are many reasons. Most have not read the Holy Quran and depend on these *ulemas* for religious guidance. And, like all religions' fountainheads, the Holy Quran is a reflecting pool. You get what you want to get - coupled with the fact that it is written in Arabic, a language alien to most Muslims in India. Does this sound familiar?

Second, you may compare Indian Muslims with people living in island nations (they speak mixed languages called Creole and follow ancient rituals) or countries with a Hindu minority (who celebrate festivals like Tai Pusam, now extinct in India). Minorities tend to cling to their old faith. It gives them an identity. They fear complete annihilation if assimilated into an Indian secular or majoritarian identity. The greater the perceived threat from the majority, the greater the tendency to seek shelter under old beliefs, ancient roots and practices. This creates a more significant schism and attracts ridicule and counterreaction. It needs sagacity, understanding and statesmanship to break this cycle.

The guy who issued a *fatwa* on Sonu Nigam is neither a maulvi authorised to issue a *fatwa* nor is his *fatwa* valid (not a religious opinion, fatwa cannot be demeaning, etc.). He is just a publicity-seeking idiot (he claims to be the 34th descendant of the Prophet - Peace be upon him). But he represents the reactionary psyche of Indian Muslims. It suits ulemas to have Indian Muslims who live in fear. It ensures their stranglehold over society.

The tragedy is that the more touchy and narrow you get, the more you are attracted to the lure of 'better Islam' - '*my interpretation is better than yours*'. And this is never-ending.

Ordinary and tolerant Muslims suffer in the meantime - no social movement, fear, violence and social distance from other communities.

II

Some time back, an advertisement made headlines for all the wrong reasons due to its religious overtone. Intrigued by the controversy, I earnestly watched the Surf Excel detergent advertisement.

Essentially, a little girl braves all the Holi (festival of colour in India) to protect a young Muslim boy from getting his white clothes dirty. She then drops him on her bicycle (Note: No carrier) to the neighbourhood mosque - for him to offer prayer - and enjoins him to participate in revelry after prayers.

The controversy erupted, as some saw religious overtones here. They juxtaposed this against another advertisement showing a Hindu getting rid of his old emaciated father at the crowded Kumbh fair (thereby showing his co-religionists in a bad light) and another advertisement of a young devout Muslim boy faithfully waking up his stone-deaf uncle for morning ablution during the holy month of fasting (thereby showing Muslims in a good light)...

Even worse was the reaction that, while Hindus play with red, some others play with the blood of innocents, which cannot be washed away.

Reaction? Boycott Surf Excel. It is anti-Hindu. Boycott is the new mantra...

I found nothing wrong with the Surf Excel advertisement. However, I would have preferred it if, instead of using a religious tone (knitted cap, mosque steps, etc.), the girl had protected a young lad who was scared of watercolours and was trying to avoid getting his new white dress dirty.

Why stereotype Muslims - even small kids - as religiously devout?

And do you want someone who deserts his ageing parents to be part of your religion? Just shun him, even in an advertisement. He does not belong to an inwards-looking, egalitarian religion like Hinduism.

We cannot have a world where everything is to one's liking. And one is supersensitive to one's beliefs, faith and predilections. We should perceive things in perspective - as a package - not in isolation. Not being reactionary.

I have many issues with *'The Hindu'* for their motivated coverage (my view) of the Rafael deal. But I have not stopped subscribing to the paper. Being broad-minded is being inclusive, and being a democrat means allowing for dissent and differences.

How important is religion in our lives?

Animals do not follow any religious dictum. But they follow their own rules - social constructs - mainly for survival. For example, hardly any animal kills its kind and eats. Social biology, right?

As we evolved, we needed a bigger brain to survive. As our brains grew, we created complex societies, economies and religions. Organised religion is purely a human construct. It is the outcome of the cognitive revolution. It is intersubjective, widely held 'make belief', not an objective reality.

So, religion comes AFTER humanity. Right?

It is okay to be religious. But indeed, a part of our expanded cranium can host what is innately human - love, compassion, togetherness, empathy, forgiveness, empathy...

Can we not be human first?

'An eye for an eye shall make all of us blind.' Said a man. (Mahatma Gandhi)

In return, we pumped two bullets into him. Ironically, the outcome of our scientific revolution was used to silence the voice of reason and humanity.

74

Triple Talaq

Marry and do not divorce; the throne of Allah shakes due to divorce.
- The Hadith of Prophet Muhammad (peace be upon him)

I was watching a fascinating TV debate between a section of oppressed Muslim women and the status quoists represented by the Muslim personal law board, *ulemas* and religious scholars, all men.

The women had complaints about domestic violence, polygamy, triple *talaq* and non-payment of maintenance. Some had horror stories such as triple *talaq* by post, SMS, WhatsApp or phone. Or triple *talaq* in one sitting. Most were from modest backgrounds and were left to fend for themselves, very vulnerable and bitter.

The defence centred around the following points.

a) Islam treats men and women as equals. Even in polygamy, men have to treat all wives equally

b) There is a defined procedure for *talaq*, recommending a month's gap between each uttering and efforts to reconcile.

c) Islam looks down upon triple *talaq*, and the Prophet (may peace be upon him) cursed men who gave triple talaq in one sitting.

d) Many examples from the audience related to domestic violence and had nothing to do with triple *talaq*.

e) Personal law is an integral part of the protection given to minorities in India. The Holy Quran is the edifice of Muslims, and its wordings and injunctions cannot be diluted. *Talaq*, indeed, the entire personal law, derives its genesis from the Holy Quran. If someone has a grievance, one should reach out to community elders (read *ulemas*) for a solution.

As the debate heated up, women accused the scholars of being bigoted and willing accomplices in such practices. The other side accused the women of being planted, not faithful and possibly non-Muslim to show Islam in a bad light.

I changed the channel. The communication was broken.

During the entire debate, I did not get answers to two fundamental questions that I have asked many Muslim friends.

1) If triple *talaq* is terrible (and cursed), what punishment has been prescribed for men who resort to it? Has anybody been punished for this?

2) If triple *talaq* and polygamy are so fundamental to religion, how come over 22 major Islamic nations, including Saudi and Pakistan, have declared it illegal?

I reflect that while Muslim women are yearning for equality, not in empty words but also in action, the theocrats and revivalists are unwilling to go beyond shibboleth, rabble-rousing and canards.

I do not doubt that Islam is a great religion with billions of faithful who have embraced it by persuasion or power. But it has also been misused by those with the power to do this. Most religious leaders and political powers are men. Otherwise, the religion will face resistance and fissures from within. You cannot ignore the voice of half the faithful and prosper.

Meanwhile, as a state, it is time for the nation of India to say triple *talaq* to antiquated and anachronous practices that discriminate against women, such as triple *talaq* and polygamy.

II

Meanwhile, the All India Muslim Personal Law Board has developed new guidelines for *talaq*. According to these new guidelines, at least a month should occur between each utterance. Triple *talaq* in one session is not illegal, but it is not desirable and can lead to social ostracisation. Of course, they have reaffirmed that courts have no locus standi in this issue.

It is not clear what locus AIMPLB has in this matter. For records, it is an NGO set up in 1972. Shia Muslims have a different board. Women activists have set up another board. So, AIMPLB represents Sunni Muslim men, at best. Could you let it be as it is? It is for the Apex court to adjudicate on the issue.

My Muslim friends have stressed in the past that in Islam, there should be at least a six-month gap between each utterance. Does this mean that AIMPLB has gone against Qur'anic injunctions?

The fact remains that the Board represents orthodox Muslim men who benefit from outdated practices such as easy talaq, no need to pay maintenance and multiple marriages.

Social ostracisation is nonsense in the current day and age.

What locus standi do I have in the matter? A lot. It is a matter of gender justice and pure humanity. Muslim women are my country's women, and I have all the right to articulate issues of injustice.

It is not a community issue to the exclusion of courts. The board has fallen too short of minimum expectations. It needs to be dissolved.

III

Despite all the criticism it attracts - and rightfully so - about being unequal, cruel, and inhuman, the *talaq* system (mind you, not triple *talaq* in one sitting) has one great advantage. It allows for the quick dissolution of unhappy marriages and enables partners to pick up the threads and rebuild their lives afresh.

This luxury is not available in secular personal law, especially to Hindus. If a marriage is to be dissolved by consensus, it takes a few years to annul. If one party is unwilling, it may take well over a decade. Ultimately, it is bitterness and a waste of the best part of life in court. And this applies to both sides. If one is unlucky, one faces a *dowry* harassment case in a criminal court. Court proceedings are tortuous and add more bitterness to your life, including opening up all aspects of your private life in the open.

The problem's origins lie in the unequal distribution of wealth (patrimony). Deeply patriarchal Hindu society allows succession and inheritance along male lines, and daughters either get limited *streedhan*, a lavish marriage at most, and at times *dowry* (now banned and hence, usually hidden). It is unequal for parents as they end up spending disproportionately on their daughter's marriage at times.

This lack of financial security for women, coupled with taking up the role of homemaker, makes women very insecure. And society does not take kindly to those who have a broken marriage. The result is that women bear it out, even in the face of domestic violence and general incompatibility.

This applies to some men also. I know of cases where men are the victims and are in constant fear of *dowry* harassment.

This is precisely why society, including courts, tries to convince couples to try to make up and allow dissolution only as a last resort. In the end, it is a bitter, life-changing battle.

In Western society, wealth is equally divided upon the dissolution of marriage. The total wealth minus less inheritance on either side is divided. This has led to another problem. The dissolution of marriage is so financially ruining that the institution of marriage is in decline. It has nearly disappeared in many societies. Men and women live together, produce and raise babies, but never get married officially. You would be surprised that it is common to use 'My Woman' rather than 'My Wife.'

That is a case of overcorrection.

So, when we talk of a uniform civil code, we should not restrict ourselves to discussing the Muslim practices of *talaq* and Polygyny. It should also address the Hindu practices of inheritance, ease of marriage dissolution, and protection of the very institutions on which a healthy society is built.

IV

While invalidating triple *talaq* among Indian Muslims is a significant step forward, the Indian Supreme Court has missed a considerable opportunity to usher in gender justice. To that extent, this judgement is not at the same level as the American Declaration of Independence or the French age of entitlement regarding profundity or social impact. Possibly, the highest court believed that

India was still not ready for a significant leap.

What was disappointing was that the honourable judges looked for answers within religious texts and did not interpret and define gender equality in terms of the current religion called humanism.

Let us examine the linkage between politics, society, family and religion.

Politics deals with the affairs of the state. Even in a democracy, citizens are only notionally involved in politics. Politics touches our lives daily through its organs: the executive, legislature, and judiciary. Politics represents the most prominent society, where most citizens participate as individuals and interest groups.

Society is a generic term and may consist of a small or large number of people. Humanity itself is a society. But most of us spend our lives in a small society - city, village, neighbourhood, apartment complex, etc. We care most about society, especially its censure, opprobrium, support, and collective consciousness. Note how politics has made inroads into society, e.g., through Panchayats and Ward councils.

Family is the four walls and caters to our emotional needs. What happens within four walls must remain within four walls is an adage. Just observe how the State has made inroads into our family affairs. A classic case is the personal law dealing with marriage, divorce, inheritance, and death. Interestingly, it is the liberal humanists who are egging the State on to invade more and more into family affairs—for example, marital rape, child abuse etc.

Where does religion fit in?

Religion is a deeply personal affair. Within a family, one may be religious; others may be notionally religious. Whom (if at all) you pray is your personal affair.

So, how does the state and its operating part - the politics - invade your religious space?

Initially, religion developed in a vacuum and was just a set of beliefs - a way of life. Look at Hinduism (*Sanatan Dharma*, ever-present, literally), Judaism, etc. You could not adopt a religion. You were born into it; it embraced you completely, yet you were unaware of it. Even the history books hardly talk about the religious faith of ancient people, including the ruling class.

The ruling class saw the need for religious sanctions to justify their entitlement and divinity. They created, propagated and used the faith that suited them. Even then, the earlier religions, viz. Buddhism and Jainism were not very interested in the politics of the State. These were more inward journeys and not expansionists. They did not need the crutches of the State.

Only the proselytising and congregational religions needed State support to expand. They were not growing in isolation. Existing religions were set, and they had no virgin ground to harness. They needed to show their worth, and overt signs such as congregations, pantheon, text, codification, State funding, and military support helped them in their quest.

But politicians would extract their price, so politics started invading an individual's intensely private domain: religion.

An extreme case is a theocratic state, where the state demands that people have a specific religious faith and pray in a particular manner.

In the current context, it is anachronous, especially in a secular polity.

Hence, I am disquieted about the court delving into religious texts to find answers to societal, family, and individual questions.

V

There seems to be sharp polarisation on the issue of the (instant) Triple Talaq bill (*Talaq-a-Biddat*, something even the Holy Quran looks down on), which was introduced in parliament yesterday and is expected to be passed today.

In essence, this bill provides for 3 years imprisonment for instant triple *talaq*, makes it non-bailable (meaning, due process needs to be followed to get bail), provides for immediate subsistence to the wife (to be granted by a magistrate) and provides for custody of minor children to wife.

Triple *talaq* has generated much heat and traction, especially after the split verdict of the Supreme Court striking down the practice. It is already proscribed in most Islamic nations. The apex court decision emboldens the Government of the day, and politically, it sees it as an opportunity to split the Muslim votes along gender lines and also between forward-looking and obscurantist Muslim males.

If we were to analyse the objections to the bill, these stem from the following.

1) It has been drafted quickly and should be referred to the parliament select committee. This argument has some merit, as laws affecting society must be deliberated well and all parties heard adequately, including the most regressive ones, like the All India Muslim Law Board (AIMLB). This is the essence of democracy

2) The bill infringes upon the religious freedom of the Muslim minority. The Supreme Court has settled this issue. The instant *talaq* is invalid, and the bill only provides punishment for its violation. Do remember, after rendering it illegal too, scores of triple *talaq* have been witnessed, including for bizarre and trivial reasons.

3) It prevents any chance of reconciliation, as the husband, once jailed, will not reconcile. This is untrue, as bail can be obtained from the court, and the case can be withdrawn if reconciliation happens. Jail is the end process, not the beginning of the process. It at least puts a fear of law in one's mind.

4) It will render women and minors more vulnerable. I could not understand the logic at all. I mean, nothing is more vulnerable for women than to be divorced on flimsy grounds and rendered homeless in the dead of a cold winter night (and go through the shameful process of *Nikah Halala* - getting married to and consummate with another Muslim man before being admitted by original husband)

5) This is a conspiracy to imprison millions of Muslim males. This is fearmongering. Are you telling the nation that millions of Muslim males resort to instant *talaq*? Of course, like any law, this can be misused, but courts and remedies are available

6) This began an attempt to bring about the Uniform Civil Code. Today, it is instant triple *talaq*; tomorrow, it will be *Nikah Halala*,

then bigamy....Muslims are being deprived of their law. I find this logic shameful. *Nikah Halala* and bigamy should have gone decades back. We are at least 3 decades behind most Islamic nations, which are themselves not precisely showcases of progressive thinking by any stretch of the imagination. This regressive practice should go.

What is especially galling is that the same organisations (AIMPLB- which is a self-styled custodian of Muslim rights. It has no legal sanctity but gets a disproportionate share on air) who have worked for decades trampling upon the just rights of Muslim women and only catered to the ultra-orthodox males, are crying foul.

They maintained studied silence for decades when middle-aged and old Arabs from the Middle East, including those on medical visas, were descending (and continue to do so) at Hyderabad to marry poor young, hapless Muslim girls aged 12 to 18 to satisfy their lust for a brief period and then leave them in the lurch after instant triple *talaq*, all solemnised (and arranged) by a local *Qazi*. Remember, this has been happening since the infamous case of Amina came to light in the eighties and continues to date.

All unjust and exploitative practices should go, irrespective of religion. This bill should be just a beginning, not an end in itself.

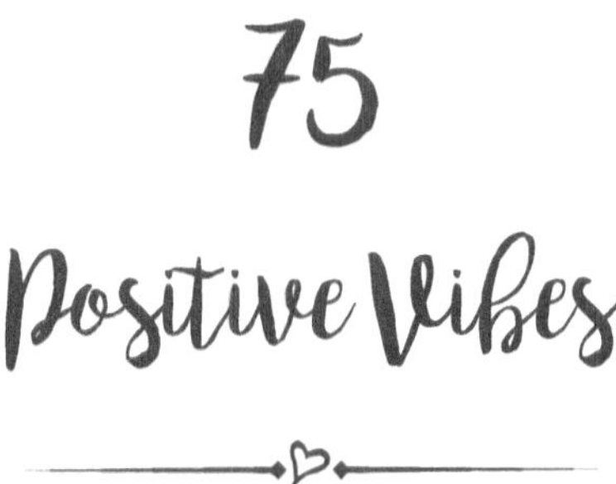

75

Positive Vibes

Choose to be optimistic, it feels better.
- Dalai Lama

'Think positive and positive shall happen.'
'We are what we think'
'Right thinking leads to right actions.'

You have heard similar messages so often in your life.

True to our tradition of subtle messages through stories, we have been taught about Dikpals—the directional guardian Gods—who constantly chant *'Astu'*, only occasionally breaking into *'Thatasthu,'* meaning what you wish shall happen.

While we sat on their laps on starry nights on their terrace, our grandparents taught us that we should always talk positively, as no one knows when the Gods will utter *Thathastu*. Anything negative we think or utter at that time will happen.

Speak positive, bear no evil.....

All civilisations speak about it, and all religions do, too. These lead to what we call *'Universal Values'*—helpful, forgiving, charitable, gentle, honest, truthful, kind, righteous, full of piety, etc.

The purpose was simple: to make life livable, to make our life experience positive, to fill us with hope and energy, to trust others, and to be trustworthy.

But do we all practice even a fraction of what wisdom we received or what we think is right?

I was exchanging notes with my friends in different parts of the world when, to my shock, I learned that the answer was a resounding 'NO'.

Politicians have been known to speak ill of adversaries, trade in fear and division, and see only the negative aspects of their adversaries...

But what about the rest of us?

The media is full of negatives. Television serials' stories revolve around promiscuity, plotting, black magic, superstitions, violence, and vitriol. And their attire is gaudy, too.

An event is not newsworthy unless it is negative and engenders anger, not to mention highly divisive, high-pitched TV debates.

We bring violence even in sports headlines. *'India mauls Pakistan in hockey.'*

Social media is as divisive as it could be. We are to blame, as it is a purely democratic forum run by the people.

Except for occasional positive messages, which, mercifully, get forwarded faster than negative news. This indicates our exasperation with negatives and yearning for positives.

We want our children to lead better lives than ours, and this means giving them more hope for the future. But are we doing it? Are we not engendering more hatred, disillusionment, a sense of purposelessness, and depression?

Ironically, our generation did not suffer from any of these. We have more comforts than any generation in human history, we have less to fear from epidemics (the African ebola outbreak killed only a fraction of what was killed each year due to the plague in Europe), we have less to fear of despots, tyranny, human rights violations, and oppression, we do not fear nuclear annihilation, we have largely bridged the information asymmetry, and society is less hungry and more equal than ever...

In our personal lives, we are paid better than our parents, have a better work environment, and have better working terms overall.

We should thank the previous generations for this. From steam engines to aircraft, medicine to inoculation, and agricultural research to the Internet, we are reaping the benefits of their research and sagacity.

Most of the problems we face are created by us—global warming, pollution, discord, wars, migration...

Are we leaving our planet and our children better off than we inherited?

They say, 'You reap what you sow.'

Tragically, the fruits are reaped by the next generation. Our toxic seeds will pollute the lives of our children and grandchildren. And we love them, don't we?

And that is the irony.

P.S. This write-up was written before the COVID-19 pandemic.

76

Lord Rama

Abandon pride, which is the same as Tamas-guna (darkness), rooted as it is in ignorance and is a source of considerable pain; and adore Lord Shri Rama, the Chief of the Raghus and an ocean of compassion.
- Saint Tulsidas

Something fascinating about the stories of Lord Rama is that He is revered not only in India but also over large areas spanning from Thailand to Mauritius.

And it has nothing to do with whether He was a God or mere human, a mythological figure or a historical one, or whether a temple should be built at the exact spot where he was born. Far beyond it, far more profound is the persona of Lord Rama and awe-inspiring stories, written across centuries in different parts of Asia and transmitted across generations in other languages.

I am a very small person and not a scholar, even to attempt to fathom the messages. However, there are specific values that I can see woven into stories about Lord Rama.

He was the most inclusive personality and represented the Indian was of open arm embrace. Remember His ready acceptance of different tribes, races and even animals and creating a cohesive group to fight for a just cause. His favourite disciple, Hanuman, was possibly tribal but was the closest to Him—a message for us Indians about how liberal our Gods were.

Lord Rama recognised love above rigour and the concept of 'touch me not', which became the bane of Hinduism in later years. His accepting half-eaten ber fruits from Shabari is one of the most beautiful stories one can read. Or his performing last rites for even a bird, Jatayu, who laid down his life in service of the Lord. Love and Noble intent transcend all caste, creed, and cleanliness boundaries.

And His respect for elders, obedience, and acceptance of suffering for self and wife to fulfil His father's words. I am unsure how many among us would undertake even a tiny fraction of what He undertook out of sheer love for His parents.

But beyond that, He held no rancour or acrimony against His stepmother, brothers and even His enemy. He ensured that slain enemy soldiers received proper respect in death.

Lord Rama respected knowledge and accepted the superior knowledge of His arch-enemy, Ravana, by inviting him to conduct rituals to pray to Shiva.

Or His righteous conduct as a king, whereby conscious of public criticism, He lets go of His pregnant wife. His Dharma as a king was higher than His as a family man and loving husband. Is there any parallel in today's world?

As I told you, Lord Rama's life and stories teach us many timeless virtues and values. However, the one that touches me most is a lesser-known story.

After the demon king Ravana was slain, Lord Rama was sitting on a rock, pensive, flanked by his brother and his generals. In the meantime, Mandodari, the queen and wife of Ravana, approached the battlefield upon hearing about the death of her invincible and immortal husband. Full of rage, she planned to question or even punish Lord Rama. She came from behind, her hair open and flying, the afternoon sun shining bright behind her.

Lord Rama sees a shadow approaching Him and recognises that it is feminine. He just moves away lest His own shadow overlap with hers.

I just wanted to let you know that no words were exchanged. Mandodari stops in her tracks. She is knowledgeable. She understands. She recognises the greatness of Lord Rama. A person who would not even take the space of a shadow, who could not let even His shadow touch another woman's...And she was wailing about a king who had forcibly abducted the wife of Lord Rama. And Lord Rama had no rage, no feeling of retribution. Only respect...

Now, in the contemporary liberal world, this story may seem antediluvian. Our standard of morality and trust has changed significantly.

But for Maryada Purushottam, every action was to inspire countless generations of humanity. He was conscious of his stature as a role model and conscience keeper of Dharma and good behaviour, and he could accept personal sorrow and suffering for that.

That made Lord Rama great. That made Aryavarta the beacon of hope for humanity. That made Lord Rama encapsulate all that is innately Indian. He was Indianness and our values personified.

Let us pray this Ramnavami that we will live by Lord Rama's ideals. His temple should be in our hearts.

Happy Ramnavami !!

P.S. This story was written before the grand Lord Rama Lala temple was built at Ayodhya

77

Anxiety

Our anxiety does not empty tomorrow of its sorrows, but only empties today of its strengths
- C.H. Spurgeon

'Live in the present, Mr Dewalla. And stop worrying about the future,' my friend Sabina told me during a long-distance conversation.

I had spent half a day at a hospital, getting my mother checked by a couple of doctors and was expressing how worried I was about her health and what the future held for me.

Have I not heard it before? My favourite is Swami Chinmayananda's golden words while explaining a Shloka from the Bhagavad Gita: "We dissipate energy through the burden of the past, feverish excitement in the present, and anxiety about the future."

I guess all religions have cautioned about excessive anxiety about the future and warned against carrying the guilt of the past.

All wise men warn against worrying about the future. 'Anxiety is the punishment we endure for the sins we might or might not commit in the future'. Eckhart Tolle, who has written an immensely illuminating book titled 'The Power of Now', advocates living in the present and being constantly aware.

Are humans the only creatures who worry about the unforeseen future or the immutable nature of the past?

During my evening stroll yesterday, I saw the building kids playing and fawning over the resident cats. They offered cat food in a plastic tiffin box and water in a tumbler. The cats seemed smug with the attention they were receiving. But did it cross their minds that this attention may be short-lived or that they may not get this attention or the delicious food the next day? Unlikely.

Do animals carry regrets from their past and worry about the future? Animals do learn from their past mistakes. I have seen cats or dogs being extra careful after a precipitous fall. We call it learning. Do lame cats or dogs regret their hastiness leading to their coming under the wheel of some bike? I do not think their memory retains it for so long.

Have you seen a cat leap for a bird? It does meticulous planning with mathematical accuracy before leaping. Of course, it is intuitive. But does it worry about getting injured before it embarks? Or worry, who would take care of it should it get injured? Again, unlikely. Not because cats have nine lives. It is just that they live in their immediate present.

So, is anxiety a purely human phenomenon? And, because we have no control over the future, we have created religion and even God. Or, as scriptures tell, God created humans and placed them at the apex of His creation so that they could think, understand the true nature of God, praise God and seek salvation from the cycle of rebirths? No one knows.

But I am sure, if our domestic cats were to worry about the future, they would have spawned a rudimentary religion of a sort with a cat cult, too.

Probably, the cats do not worry, as they know they will get something to fill their stomachs tomorrow. And if it happens, other things do not matter. But isn't it true for most of us, too? Indeed, most of us do not have to worry about our livelihood and the basic comforts of life. But it is not enough.

No, I do not carry too much of a burden of my past - occasional what-ifs, especially in academics, choice of profession, relationships or investment decisions. More often, I reminisce about the pleasant things of the past, which is not such a bad thing.

And frankly, for my present, I have handed over the reins in His hands. I flow like a log in the swollen river, riding a roller coaster in the current, moving towards the sea, where we all shall arrive one day.

But I do worry about my future – a lonely one, if not a miserable one.

Over the next few days, God willing, I shall explore and dive deep into my anxieties to seek amelioration.

I am already worried about my long day tomorrow!

P. S. Also, the cats got no attention the next day as the kids were busy, but they seemed unconcerned. They did not have to worry about tomorrow. When it comes, it comes. How it comes does not matter. Eckhart Tolle would be happy.

78

Anniversary of Merging with Eternity

To forget one's ancestors is to be a brook without a source, a tree without a root.

- Chinese Proverb

I recently observed the annual ritual related to my father's merging with eternity. He left us eleven years ago, but the memory of *Nayna* is still fresh in our minds. I remember him every day in some way.

Every anniversary, I experience an emotional roller coaster as the associated rituals symbolise the arrival of the departed soul and the arrival of the forefathers to receive the oblation. First, the oblation is offered to the fire, then to the Gods and then to the Brahmins, who represent our forefathers. We provide new clothes to the Brahmins, wash their feet, seek their blessings, and offer them meals and Dakshina.

Most Hindu families observe anniversaries, though the rituals may differ from one community or region to another. In the strictest sense, monthly rituals, or rituals on every no-moon day, must be observed and offered during the *Pritru Paksha* (a designated fortnight around October). In addition, on the *Mahalya day*, all forefathers are remembered, and oblations are offered. Typically, in a patrilineal society, the sons observe it, though daughters have a role too, such as cooking and serving while observing strict penance.

As I was following the ritual, under the guidance of the priest, I observed that during the ritual, one remembered the departed soul and two earlier generations. The rest of the ancestors are clubbed generically as forefathers.

It got me thinking about the significance of the ritual.

As a starting point, I considered it man's eternal question for immortality. Let me explain. Once a person leaves, one is remembered less and less often during conversation, and gradually, the memory of the person fades away. We want to be remembered, at least for a few more generations - a temporary immortality. I am chuckling at this oxymoron. Why only three generations? Because one has, at most, direct or vicarious tales and memories of three generations. Beyond that are all fables, make-believes and romanticised accounts of ancestry.

But were our ancestors so eager to be remembered? Remember, Hinduism is all about seeking salvation – *Mukti*. Who wanted to carry baggage, including the burden of being remembered? Therefore, the anniversary could not be due to selfish motives of being remembered in the future.

In many communities, I realised that daily oblation, in the form of water *tarpan*, is offered to Gods, Sages, and Ancestors. These are called '*Rins*' (debts) and relate to debt of birth, debt of ancestry, and debt of birth, respectively. It is believed that they live in different *Lokas* (worlds). We owe our existence to our parents. Therefore, it made sense to remember them even after their departure.

Interestingly, Hindus are not the only ones who remember their ancestors and observe their anniversaries. I gather that Muslims, too, observe it through prayers and gatherings.

Many tribal societies have elaborate rituals for remembering the dead and believe the deceased has never left the family.

I watched an animated movie called 'Coco', which depicts another world of the dead. If descendants do not remember a dead person for a particular period, the dead person moves from the afterlife to the netherworld.

What surprises me is that some form of ancestor remembrance and worship was observed in societies worldwide in all known eras.

Did our ancestors discover something, independently and without the benefit of communication across geographies, about the existence of another world and the need to be in touch and propitiate the ancestors? If this is not done, something equal to '*Pitru dosha*' (curse of the ancestor) will befall.

Modern science does not believe in it. But tradition does. Who knows what the truth is?

Meanwhile, I remembered *Nayna* all day yesterday and today and was happy to receive him for a few hours, even if symbolically. It was not due to any fear of the unknown befalling me but for the genuine warmth that his memory brings, and I wanted to thank him from the bottom of my heart for my existence, sustenance, values, and everything that I am today.

79

Love And Not Hate

You are here to enable the divine purpose of the Universe to unfold. That is how important you are!
- Eckhart Tolle

I watched this incredible video of Dr. B.M. Hegde, a cardiologist and educator better known as a rebel doctor, for his contrarian views on modern medical sciences, the causes of diseases, and treatment regimes.

One statement that struck me right at my rib cage was how our cells resonate with all other cells in the universe.

The Professor says that each of our trillions of body cells is a body in itself, with its own consciousness and specific role in the body. Each cell receives part of universal consciousness through its antenna. Cells of other human beings also get their sustenance from the same universal consciousness.

Each cell resonates with other cells and cooperates with others. It does not distinguish between cells in our body and those in other bodies. It exudes positivity, cooperation, and love.

We train our cells to distinguish by superimposing our thoughts, prejudices and accumulated experience.

To achieve this, we need to create reasons to hate - religion, gender, colour, race, political outlook, language, looks...Love needs no such force. It is natural.

When we train our cells to hate relentlessly, they start hating not only the cells in other bodies but also their own. The result is autoimmunity, diseases, sickness, and degradation.

Be as it is. It can not be disputed that if we learn to hate, it devours ourselves first. Negativity multiplies negativity manifold.

One such example is the constant bombardment of hate messages on social media. I, too, was not immune to its deleterious effects until I shut myself off from such groups, people, and messages. I stopped watching news channels, as they peddled only negativity. And trust me, I am much calmer, more positive, and more energetic.

Try it.

I would dare say that our current economic mess and social unrest are due to the proliferation of too many negative and hateful messages on our phones, laptops, and TVs, invading our minds. We are training our social fabric to be torn by hate. And it starts with us hating ourselves at the very cellular level.

Why did this video resonate so much with me?

Well, I am reading Bhagavad Gita these days and the same evening, I was reading verse 7 from Chapter 13

This chapter deals with knowledge of *ksetra* (our body) and *khetragya* (knower of body). In this verse, the Lord describes the Gyani (knowledgeable/wise) as possessing.

अमानित्वमदम्भित्वमहिंसा क्षान्तिरार्जवम् |

आचार्योपासनं शौचं स्थैर्यमात्मविनिग्रह:

Amanitvam adambhitvam ahimsa ksantir arjavam

Acaryopasanam saucam sthairyam atmavinigrahah

[Humility, unpretentiousness, non-injury, forgiveness, straightforwardness, teacher service, purity, steadfastness, and self-control.]

Each word has been explained in great detail. Is it not a profound understanding?

233

80
Maha Kumbh 2025

❦

At the Kumbh Mela, we are reminded that every soul is interconnected, and our collective journey is towards enlightenment.
- Anonymous

It is believed that every pilgrimage is a divine calling. One can only earnestly desire a pilgrimage and then watch in total surrender and humility as things unfold.

For the last month or more, I have been seeing the clippings, watching the news, and reading about Maha Kumbh 2025 at the Sangam (confluence) of the Ganga, Yamuna, and Saraswati (invisible) rivers. I desired to participate in this 'once in 144 years' event, but it never seemed feasible.

And then, suddenly, one fine morning, the calling came. After a brief conversation with my brother Parthasarthy, who agreed to come down and take care of Amma, I started looking for flight tickets. Nothing was available. If I found one, I would get a 'regret' message when I clicked the 'Pay Now' button.

After much frustration and disappointment, I nearly gave up. And it happened in just a flash. Reeta, my sister, advised me to check via Kolkata. Lo and Behold, it was available if one booked separate flights. It was expensive, though.

Nevertheless, tickets were booked for 17 February, and I would return on 19 February. I had a whole week to undertake the penance and soak in the religiosity. Parthasarthy, too, booked his tickets to come to Bangalore and take care of Amma in my absence.

A day before I left for Prayagraj via Kolkata, our neighbour Pratibahji and I completed the *Parayana* (recitation) of Valmiki's Ramayana and carried out a small *Udyapan* (culmination) prayer. It had taken us just under six months to read aloud 24,000 *shlokas* (verses) in Amma's presence, correcting pronunciation errors and minding *Sandhis* (word joins) and *Samasas* (compounding) on the way.

II

I was already tired when I completed the security protocols at the Bangalore airport. I had not disclosed to Amma or Partha that I was running a slight temperature - possibly due to anxiety and anticipation. I wondered if it was because I was not travelling often these days, the airport was busier now, and security was more invasive & strict, or the age was catching up with me. Till a few years back, travelling was second nature to me. And, if I was tired due to age, what about those much older? How do they travel? Age spares no one. I lamented that not much is thought about convenience or even the quality of life of elders.

My mind raced back to Amma. She must have completed her dinner and prepared to sleep. I was sure Partha kept her company with his witty conversation and engaging mannerisms.

The flight was mostly on time, and on the flight, I had a cold *Vada Pav* offered by the airlines since I declined the option of dinner at the Kolkata guest house, which I would reach around midnight. This turned out to be a big mistake. I took a taxi to the guesthouse, and after some difficulty locating it, I checked in to catch a few hours of sleep. It was well past midnight now. My trouble started the moment I lay down. The air conditioner was not working properly, and mosquitos seemed to relish the blood of the new guest. I had a troubled sleep, and a stomach bug hit me early in the morning. It became so bad that I could not even digest water. I gave up drinking water without checking for a nearby loo to save embarrassment.

I took a taxi to the airport early in the morning and reached it in time. Kolkata airport is large and modern, but it was reasonably crowded and quite chaotic. After using the men's facilities, I boarded the flight to Prayagraj. It would be an hour-long flight, and I would reach there by eleven.

After settling in my seat, I observed the passengers around me. There were people of all age groups. Lots of Marwadi families and chatty and ebullient groups. Some even had their domestic staff to support them at Prayagraj. Some elderly Bengalis were worried about whether the taxi would fetch them or not. The gentleman behind me was really old and toothless and insisted on sitting in the aisle seat, as he had to go to the toilet often. I wondered how inconvenient and difficult it must be to plan, let alone complete this arduous pilgrimage. My mind raced back to Amma. She must have had her wash and breakfast and preparing to lie down to give some rest to her tired limbs. Amma is ninety-three, is wheelchair-bound due to old age, has hip injuries and Parkinson's, and is dependent on a caretaker for all her activities of daily living. Amma is very perceptive and blessed me before I left for the pilgrimage. But she hardly spoke, and I wondered if she even remembered where I had gone.

The flight was uneventful, and I could take a couple of sips of water, use the toilet, and wait for the flight to land. It hovered over for a full sixty minutes before landing. There was significant air traffic congestion, and later, I read that some 250 flights landed and took off from the tiny airport that particular day.

III

Partha's colleague Shivam was waiting on his bike at the airport as agreed. I pillion rode with my backpack sandwiched between Shivam and me. The airport and the roads had undergone a significant upgrade. Pink stone pillars on either side of the road and impressive archways greeted us. But very soon, I realised that the back carrier was pushing against my pelvic bone, and it started getting inconvenient. When we took the first of the many new road flyovers, the carrier rod would pound against my pelvis every time the bike hit the road. Somehow, bridge joints are never appropriately laid in India, and a ride over them is never without jerks. I was to travel twenty kilometres to the Sangam, and this was just the beginning.

I was impressed with the cleanliness and preparations, especially the long flyovers all over the city. If Kolkata was painted blue and white, the colour of the ruling dispensation there, Allahabad, was predictably soft shades of saffron and grey-white. Prayag was much cleaner than Bangalore, and I could not see garbage heaps anywhere.

After some distance, after the road merged with the road coming from major railheads, I could see vehicular traffic snarls and pedestrians, all leading to the Sangam. There were thousands of people, all walking purposefully. Men and women carrying small bags over their heads, reluctant children being literally dragged while they looked sideways, some small kids riding on the shoulder of father or mother, disabled men who needed to hold their knees with every step, old men bent over or bent sideways, some on wheelchairs, some carrying sticks... *Aabal, Vruddh, Naari* (kids, old and women) all in the giant procession. There were pilgrims on pushcarts, goods-carrying vehicles, three-wheelers, motorised rickshaws - any mode of transport which could take them forward and afford some rest to the tired limbs was kosher. There were orange electric shuttle buses moving pilgrims from one place to another.

Prayagraj has a rich history of freedom struggle, and after Delhi, this is the only place where roads are named after freedom fighters and literary figures. We crossed the expansive university campus and went around Alfred Park, where freedom fighter Chandrashekhar Azad was martyred. The crowd kept increasing all the time. In some corners, Finolex was distributing fluorescent yellow sun caps. Beyond this point, one could only see a sea of fluorescent yellow moving in either direction, creating some kind of wave. A young, ash-smeared, curly-haired *sadhu*, donning a marigold garland to hide his privates, caught my attention.

The entire stretch was full of billboards and flex boards, with Modiji and Yogiji looking benevolently and wishing the pilgrims well. Corporate social messages and best wishes from local leaders were also on display. Essentially, billboards jostled against one another to grab your eyeballs.

At some point, traffic restrictions were in place. There were barricades, and only vehicles with passes were allowed. But then, 'Pass' is a government construct for giving privileges. The unwashed and the impecunious do not care for any pass and would, therefore, not make way for any vehicle with the pass. The result? Incessant honking from all sides. The matter was made worse by bike taxis and goods carriers carrying essentials to various locations in Mela areas. I was suddenly reminded by Dinkar *'Simhasan Khali karo, ki janta aati hai* (Vacate your seat, as the subjects are coming)

Shivam could skirt these restrictions by taking dirt track, squeezing through narrow gaps of barricades, taking wrong directions, following diversions...every trick was kosher in this game of reaching the confluence. We crossed the majestic new wire-hanging bridge over Yamuna, and after one final hoodwinking of police, we were on the home run on Arail Ghat road along the river Yamuna. All this while, the bike carrier kept poking my pelvic bone, and it was hurting badly.

The original plan was to go to the guest house first, but it seemed more practical to take the dip first. Given the crowd and traffic restrictions, returning to the ghat from the guest house would have been impossible. Shivam took a turn, and we were on a sandy track covered with iron sheets. Many such temporary roads have been created, as the all-weather roads are simply inadequate to take the load.

After parking the bike along the VIP Ghat (it is only a name, no privilege here) on the river Yamuna, I rummaged through my bag and could take out a few pieces of clothes, some cash and, of course, my phone. I was ready now for my plunge of faith.

IV

Jaabo? Jaabo? (would you go?) Shivam was checking with the boatmen. Soon, negotiations were completed, and I was jumping from one boat to another, braving the sway, roll and pitch, my clothes and phone in hand, till I reached my designated boat. This was a small flat boat to carry ten pilgrims, but the avarice of men knows no bounds. We were already twelve, and the boatman was looking for more.

The boat commenced its journey, and we could see a traffic jam in the water. Boats do not have brakes; the standard protocol is to change direction and shout to avoid a collision. The bow of a ship carassed by back. Fortunately, the injury was minor.

After some twenty minutes of rowing, the colour of the water changed from dark to light, and we could see temporary jetties in the middle of the river. This was the confluence point.

Yamuna is deep and carries a lot of water. Ganga is shallower in these areas, with several sandy shoals clearly visible. One can get down in the waist-deep water at the confluence and take dips. We disembarked from the boat, changed and took a holy dip. The water seemed clean, and I could also offer oblations and chant sacred mantras, but no one pushed me. It was refreshing and pleasant. I was scared of losing my phone, but there were other pilgrims, and someone offered to take my pictures. I reciprocated. I collected some water for family members back home, especially for Amma.

The confluence is not a small point but an entire area. There is a Ghat called Sangam Ghat built on the confluence. Most people take baths at the Ghats, which are overcrowded and not very clean. In the centre of the confluence, no such jostling was needed. If everyone wanted to come to the confluence centre, arranging an adequate number of boats would be impossible. We could see kilometres of bathing ghats on either side of the confluence, teeming with millions of people.

Once I was back on my boat, minding my phone, I realised I had taken the dip, wearing my spectacles - it is part of one's body, isn't it? - and had dropped them in the water. How would I spend another twenty-four hours or more without glasses? Progressive lenses were made to order, and it was impossible to return to the city and be back again.

I explained this predicament to the boatman, who offered to help. He dived in and fetched not one but two pairs of spectacles! One was mine, and it was totally undamaged—a minor miracle. I tipped him handsomely.

Due to the boat's inertia and discomfort and the fact that it was sunny and warm, I did not change into dry clothes. Soon, we were back. We could see hundreds of boats all around us.

Overall, the bath was very satisfactory, and I felt blessed.

V

Shivam met me at the banks, and we resumed our bike journey on the undulating, temporary road, with the carrier pounding my backbone. We could see various Ghats - Arail Ghat, Sangam Ghat, etc. to our left, teeming with hundreds of thousands of pilgrims. The entire area seemed washed with red and orange colours. To our right were makeshift tent cities, *Akhadas*, congregation halls, and permanent and makeshift temples. A helipad made an appearance somewhere. And, of course, thousands were walking in all directions. At places, there were temporary dirt tracks covered with white sand and iron sheets.

Finally, we arrived at the guest house. This was a newly constructed multi-storey apartment, and it was barely furnished. But I could at least stretch my limbs. Now, I realised I was dehydrated and started developing cramps. I had not even sipped water for at least five hours. Shivam fetched some bottled water, which I had. And dysentery returned with equal ferocity. I was starving and was too tired and weak to venture out. The nearest eatery would be kilometres away. I checked the map and realised the place was called Naini. I recalled from school history that Jawaharlal Nehru was imprisoned at Naini Jail during the freedom struggle, and he wrote some memorable books during his imprisonment. I also recalled that during the Ram Mandir agitation, I, along with Amma, was stuck at Naini Railway station for ten whole hours in the early nineteen nineties due to differences between the states of Madhya Pradesh and Uttar Pradesh on the movement of kar sevaks.

Shivam left with a promise to pick me up early in the morning and drop me off at the airport.

Tired, I dozed off. In the evening, I got up, completed my *Nitya Puja* (*Sandhya Vandanam*), and did regular chanting, and I felt better. Another family staying at the guest house offered me some medicines.

Dinner arrived at nine, as the person carrying it had to walk five kilometres on foot due to traffic restrictions. I am very grateful to him for his service. Regular visits to the loo continued throughout the night.

VI

I got up early in the morning with excruciating back pain. How could I endure the pillion ride, carrying my backpack and five litres of holy water? A doctor friend offered the ultimate motivational quote: 'God tests one's commitment and devotion during pilgrimage. Be a *bahadur baccha* (brave boy). You would make it'. This friend was encouraging me and was closely watching my progress during the pilgrimage. I am eternally grateful. Every time the bike carrier poked my pelvis, I remembered this *bahadur baccha* idiom.

With renewed vigour, I embarked on my return pillion ride journey. Alas, we were stopped shortly by the police. They would not listen to any reason or pleading. Was I going to miss my flight? I prayed hard and was about to call my friends on the police high up when another minor miracle occurred. There was a change in the policeman's mind, and the barricade was lifted - only for us - to pass through. I offered my silent thanks to God, and we continued our journey.

The early morning chill had not deterred the pilgrims from approaching various bathing points. Many had already completed and were on their way back. At a distance, on the other side of the river bank, we could see the lights of the massive tent city.

We were not entirely out of uncertainty. There were a few diversions, traffic situations, and crowds unwilling to make way, but beyond the Sangam area, things started getting better.

We suffer more in our minds than in reality. I had read that the airport was chock-a-block, and I was unsure if the flight would take off in time. In fact, it was way better than regular days at airports. Once inside, I realised that I was among my 'likes'. No, not the children of privilege or those who could make it successfully to Kumbh and back. I was not alone in limping and dragging myself.

While going through security checks, I told a fellow passenger about my ordeal of losing my spectacles in Sangam and then getting them back. The lady at the counter softly whispered, '*Na jaane kis roop mein Narayan mil jaaye*' (Who knows in what form Narayan (God) will appear).

My eyes welled up. How true. Had I not felt His benevolence at various stages during the journey? In the form of Shivam, who took his time to pick me up, drop me back, and accompany me throughout? Or the boatman who retrieved my glasses? Or the guest house family who offered me medicines? Or the policeman who allowed me to pass through? Or my Doctor friend, who constantly encouraged me.

We have miracles all around us. We just need to observe them and be thankful. No two pilgrimages are the same, and every person's experience is unique and as He wishes.

I completed the procedures, and after confirming that there was a toilet nearby, I ordered coffee and settled on a chair.

VII

Why do we undertake pilgrimages, especially the arduous ones like Maha Kumbh? It is believed that a dip during a specific planetary arrangement of the constellation, which occurs every twelve years, frees one from the cycles of birth and death and helps attain *Moksha* (liberation). To achieve this eternal bliss, Hindus undertake this journey.

My mind went back to the old, infirm, sick, heavily pregnant, infants....all of those who undertook or were undertaking this pilgrimage. My travails were nothing in comparison. In fact, I was blessed with all the privileges one could imagine in the situation. If *moksha* was to be offered, many around me deserved it much more.

I was also reading that the *Sangam* water is highly polluted with large concentrations of faecal matter. This may be true, but it does not deter the faithful. Rationality, Science, and millennium-old religious beliefs do not necessarily align. Let us examine this a little more.

Let us take the concept of *Paap* (sin). Do concept of *Paap* and *Punya* (virtues) really exist beyond the universal values, such as altruism, kindness, charity, etc? Remember the song

Ye Paap hai kya, ye punya hai kya, reeton par dharm kee mohre hain
har yug mein badalte dharmon ko, kaise aadharsh banaoge

[What are these sins, what are these virtues? The seals of religion are on traditions.
How will you make ideals out of the changing religions of every age?]

Who decides what *Paap* is and what it is not? Killing an innocent animal is a sin, but for the butcher, it is a source of his livelihood.

Does something called *Karma* (fruits of action) really get attached to one? Does it determine if one attains heavenly bliss or eternally suffers the fire of hell in the afterlife? Does the afterlife really exist? Are we to return to this world and be born as different animals or humans but with different luck based on one's accumulated *Karma* in the past life? And for this supposed afterlife and next birth, we carry out penance, undertake arduous pilgrimage, observe vows, do all kinds of prayers, meditate, etc.

Can these *Karmas* be obliterated through pilgrimage and by taking holy dips?

No one knows. *Kai jane naa* (No one knows). It is just a belief.

A common blessing we receive in India is 'Aayushman Bhavah' (Have a long life). Yet, the scriptures always advise us to work for a better afterlife. We love life, remain attached to earthly possessions, and passionately love our near and dear ones, knowing fully well that this is all transient. No one is immortal. In fact, no one seeks immortality except through good deeds. Very few succeed. Only a handful of names are remembered after a few decades of leaving this earth. If at all, we seek a fulfilling life, decent health, and short morbidity, which means suffering before our ultimate departure. Science should concentrate only on improving quality of life and compressing morbidity, not prolonging life.

Scriptures extol human life. It is said that after making all other creatures, God was not satisfied because all animals were driven by instincts and could not comprehend God's beautiful creation or realise God's presence. Therefore, God created human beings, and when He saw that Humans could perceive God and could thank him and offer prayers of gratitude, He was very pleased. It is said that Knowledge (*Gyan*) can be obtained only in human birth, and therefore, even lesser Gods are keen to take birth as humans so that they can understand the ultimate better. I am not sure that God would be happy with how humans have behaved or exploited Mother Earth and killed genres of animal species just because they could perfect weapons better and organise themselves better.

Is that why we talk of a universal consciousness, a part of which appropriates our physical form to experience one facet of earthly life and thereafter merge back into the universal consciousness, enriched with the experience? This would mean that the *Prana* inside you, me, or even the animals are the same - It is just experiencing different facets. No wonder we perceive a collective consciousness in large gatherings like Kumbh or when we bow in prayers (*Sazda*), which we can not feel when we are all alone. Or even during a large meal gathering.

If human birth is superior, should one subject it to the troubles through penance and difficult pilgrimages? Should we not preserve it and nurture it?

A rider is interested in the horse only until he crosses the dense jungle. Once he reaches the destination, he is not interested in the horse. Our body is also like that horse. We should take adequate care of it, as this is the only way to attain liberation.

Sometime back, Anita, a college and a group-mate, sang a beautiful song

Tiri duniya mein jeene se to behtar hai ki mar jaayein
Wahi aansu wahi aahen wahi gham hai jidhar jaayein

.....

Are o aasman waale bata is mein bura kya hai
Khushi ke chaar jhoke gar idhar se bhi guzar jaayein

[It's better to die than to live in your world,
The same tears, the same sighs, the same sorrow wherever we go.

.....

Oh, sky-dweller, tell me, what's wrong with this?
If a few breezes of happiness pass through here as well.]

She sang beautifully, and I tried to imitate her. Every time I tried to sing, I choked. We look at the other world as a permanent residence and this world as full of misery and unworthy of living in.

Have we not heard "*Woh duniya more babul ka ghar, ye duniya sasural.*" [That world is my father's home, this world is my in-laws' house]

If this life is so miserable, why do we want to have a long life, enjoy this life and be full of regret when our time comes?

Our constant endeavour is to improve our afterlife, even if it requires undertaking troubles in this world. Is this desire propelling millions of Hindus, including old, sick, wheelchair-bound, old and infirm, to seek to make their afterlife better by taking a holy dip at *Sangam*?

Deep in my thoughts, with an empty coffee cup between my palms, I heard a minor commotion. A prominent monk named Avdheshanand Giri Ji had just arrived to board our flight. His face glowed with lifelong penance and austere life. I took his blessings and walked towards the gate to board.

81

Our Cosmic Origin

We are the representatives of the cosmos; we are an example of what hydrogen atoms can do, given 15 billion years of cosmic evolution.
- *Carl Sagan*

I read recently that many trace elements (elements found in small quantities) owe their origin to stellar objects. In other words, Earth is constantly bombarded with particles from the universe, and not all we have are sui generis—born, bonded, and metamorphosed on Earth.

Even more interesting, our human body has traces of these stellar imports. So, we have cosmic origin!

(I was telling a friend, in half jest, that we are all cannibals. We consume what we are made of. After all, all elements are made of principal particles and elementary particles, bonded together in different proportions. So, carbon in my body eats carbon in the food.)

A deeper reflection of our cosmic origin begs the question: Did our ancestors know this apriori? Did they have more remarkable perspicacity and a deeper understanding of the interplay of the cosmos and its creation? Remember, *Aham Bramhasmi* [I encapsulate the creator.]

And this is not a one-off insight. The sound of the cosmos is believed to resonate with ohm (ॐ).

Hmm!

82

Dream Analysis

I must learn the dregs of my thought, my dreams, are the speech of my soul. I must carry them in my heart, and go back and forth over them in my mind, like the words of the person dearest to me. Dreams are the guiding words of the soul.

- C.G. Jung

You would indeed acknowledge my clairvoyance if I told you that you had been chased by a thief, an animal, or something malevolent with sinister intent. But you could not escape - your feet were struck, or the saturnine object caught up faster than you could run.

And, you would hold your breath if I also told you that you found yourself in some very odd situation - A tall man in Lilliput, a short one among Giants, skin colour mismatch, or roaming around in your birthday suit. And suddenly, you realised your oddity. No one else seemed to mind, though.

Yet, this has possibly happened to you in your dream. Possibly more than once.

Relax. Most people see such dreams, some more often, some less. Yes, some dream themes are common, recurring, and annoying.

No, you are not a troubled soul....Do not trust soothsayers, gypsies and fortune tellers. You are just normal.

The question is, why do we have such common dream themes?

Some argue that the moment we are born, we get a name, a religion, a nationality, and a language. And for the rest of our lives, we end up defending them.

Come to think of it, all our lives, we have been in invisible handcuffs and shackles placed by family, society, and religion. These are mutually overlapping supersets and subsets of each other. For example, the family follows social norms and contributes to social consciousness. Religion has an overarching influence on familial practices. Sects follow different belief systems and religious nuances.

If you were to read '*Astanga Yoga*', the first two of these relate to '*Yama*' and '*Niyama*' - 'Restraints or Ethical Disciplines' and 'Observances or Positive Disciplines'.

Unlike born free animals, we are all bound by rules, which come in the way of our innate free spirit.

It can be argued, with some merit, that human beings have progressed so much only because of societal norms. I'm not sure if this is true. A lot of progress has been made through iconoclastic individuals who dared to dream differently.

You could even argue if we have indeed progressed. During our rapacious quest, we have brought planet Earth to the brink of disaster. Would we be better off with fewer conveniences but in greater harmony with nature - sustainably, with a greater variety of flora and fauna? This is debatable, though.

Yet, deep within, we are free souls. It is our '*Prarabdh*'. And in our profound sleep state, the innate free spirit wakes up and runs wild when the social guards are down.

This is part of evolution. The spirit needs to be given space and opportunity to be free and escape from suffocating rules without damaging the socio-biological balance.

Social norms of acceptable behaviour chase the freewheeling spirit.

The free spirit finds itself at odds with the current social milieu. At times, it becomes conscious of its oddity.

Do you find my theory outlandish? Then, please read the dream analyses by more evolved souls. They are no better.

QED! I just wanted to let you know that I rest my case.

249

83

Happiness

Everything has its wonders, even darkness and silence, and I learn, whatever state I may be in, therein to be content.
- Helen Keller

Upon learning that her little son failed to get a role in the school play, the mother was distraught and looked sad.

'But Amma, I have a role. It's a very exciting one. I have to sit in the crowd and clap and cheer as my classmates perform on the stage,' the young one happily chirped.

Just reflect on it. It is not the role in the stage of life or the sense of achievement that brings happiness. And, anyway, achievements do not bring lasting happiness. Not even if you have achieved what you first set out to get.

Because all such happiness is transient, once you reach it, you want to proceed further to seek more happiness. The goalpost shifts. Let me hastily add that there is nothing wrong with chasing dreams.

Seeking durable happiness through pursuing external goals is elusive and, at best, a mirage.

True happiness lies inside. One cannot 'become' happy. One can 'be' happy. And one can choose to let that happiness manifest.

It lies within. We have to just let it express itself.

One great way to be happy is to be genuinely delighted with the achievements and happiness of others—family members, colleagues, friends, members of social circles...

This should be genuine, without any tinge of jealousy. Every cell of one's body should feel happiness. When one congratulates and joins the celebrations, every cell of the body should join in.

Why should our happiness grow manifold by being happy with the happiness of others?

Spiritually, the entire universe is pervaded by one *Prana*. We are different bodies, but what lies inside us is one common *atman*. And when we celebrate the *atman* in someone else, we celebrate ours too. Every cell in our body vibrates with joy...

The same goes for living in humility, living in eternal thankfulness, by being truthful. All these elevate our atman.

I am ending this with another story.

A monk could not meditate due to constant noise and interference, which frustrated and angered him. Finally, he took a boat to the middle of a still lake and started meditating. He could sit in his meditation for several days when, suddenly, he was rudely awakened by a thud.

Very angrily, he opened his eyes. Only to find that an astray wooden plank had hit his boat.

Upon deeper thinking, he realised that no external stimuli are needed to get angry. Anger lies inside. The demon needs to be killed from the inside.

If anger could be inside, can't happiness be?

Can't we choose to be happy? Do we need external reason and stimuli to be happy?

Can't we all be like that small child? Happy with our assigned role?

84
The Time is NOW

Therefore, send not to know
For whom the bell tolls,
It tolls for thee.
- John Donne

I am very distraught by the news of the passing away of a little girl in our building. She was just nine when the cruel hand of fate snatched away the darling of her parents. She lived barely for a week after she was diagnosed with a brain tumour. She was a lovely, cherubic girl, and I often saw her playing in our building mini-playground, riding a bicycle, on the swing or just giggling away. She spent nearly all her life in our building.

She was too young to go. She had not yet begun to experience life. And at times like these, you start wondering if God is kind, fair and just. Millions of people are elderly, very sick, and have no purpose left in life. For that matter, what is my purpose in life? Or even yours? She had an entire life beckoning her.

And yet, these are the times when faith should make you submit to His will even more. We can not understand His will and his design. Just yesterday, in a social media post, someone profoundly explained worldly existence as honey at the end of a razor's edge. Honey is sweet, but the razor's edge shall cut your tongue. Should one experience the nectar or not? Is honey evil? Isn't the razor's edge and honey expressing the non-duality of experience - pain and sweetness? You can not get the sweetness without the pain of worldly existence.

Wise men tell us about the *karmic* cycle. If some tiny part of *karma* is not extinguished, one must take a short birth to live through the *karmic* cycle. But try telling this to her inconsolable parents, who lost the apple of their eyes. They would live through this all their lives. Was it ordained for them by their *karma*?

I read a beautiful couplet by Saint Malukdas

"Jaati hamari aatma, naam hamara Ram
Paanch tattva ka putla, aaye kiye vishraam."

Our identity is our soul; our name is ordained by God. Our body is a mannequin in which the Lord came and rested for a while. We have no identity of our own. And we exist due to His will only, as long as He desires

What we can explain as the will of God can be equally elegantly presented by the tyranny of statistics. Remember the law of large numbers, normal distribution, and other more rigorous statistical treatments? Well, most people will live a reasonable life, but there are outliers on either side—someone living far too long and someone, like this little one, snatched away even before she could spread her wings and start to experience life.

The problem is that humans live in the past, present and future. In one of the Gita Gyan Yagna sessions in Mumbai, Swami Chinmayananda talked about how we dissipate our energy through bickering the past, feverish excitement in the present and anxiety about the future. The past is past - it is unchangeable. One can only carry baggage or selectively carry good memories and learning. No one knows the future - not even a second before. All we have is the present; we can try to make this moment the best by being aware, alive, and attempting to be happy and make others happy. Many spiritual leaders talk about living in the present and the power of NOW.

Aren't animals much better in this regard? They live in the present. Just watch the dog on the railway platform. Does it worry where his next bread is coming from? Or who kicked it in the morning? For sure, animals grieve. A whale carried a dead calf for months. Crows, monkeys, and elephants do mourn the death of troop members. But that is a short-term phenomenon.

Humans pay the price for their developed brains and lifelong memories. The developed brain allows us to marvel at nature, praise God, remain thankful, and create societies and families. It also allows us to modify nature around us for our benefit, develop tools, collaborate, and dominate other creatures, many of whom are much larger and more powerful.

But it also leads us to retain bad memories, suffer lifelong trauma, and imagine the worst. And human life is much longer than that of most animals.

And that is where humans have to make a choice. Our time is NOW. Not a second later. Live life, bring sunshine to the lives of others around us, spread love and enjoy the warmth of the company of near and dear ones.

For her parents, unfortunately, the trauma would take long - really long to heal. Her giggles, smile, and the sunshine she spread around her shall be missed daily. Who knows what she could have done for herself, her family and society if she had grown up like everyone else?

Rest in Peace, the sweet little girl. You have gone to a better world where you could be needed more.

1) THE HOUSE UNDER A NEEM TREE - This book revisits the life and times of nearly two generations of a typical Indian family through a hundred semi-autobiographical, relatable episodic stories. From early growing-up days to entry into professional life, dreams and progression, travel, avocations, and reflections on various social-cultural aspects, it is a subtle commentary on more than four decades of transition India has witnessed. The book is available on Notion Press, Amazon India, and Kindle.

2) MEMOIRS OF R D SAMARTH - Author- Dr R.D. Samarth. Dr. R. D. Samarth retired as a General Manager at New India Assurance Company Limited. This autobiography, published posthumously, is a recollection of his experiences in various postings and his association with people. It makes for very engrossing read, as he has covered minute details in a simple conversational style. It gives a deep insight into the socio-political life in various places where he worked, the efforts he and his team undertook to grow the Company's operations and the goodwill earned by the company due to the sheer hard work done by its professionals. The author compiled the writing and published it as a tribute to Dr. Samarth. The book is available on Notion Press and Amazon India.

3) BECOMING FARAH—Author: Farah Rustom. This astonishing, frank, and unique story is about a Parsi woman who was the first to undergo gender reassignment surgery, in 1976, and later migrated to the United States. The author enabled the publication through a detailed review and technical support. The book is available on Amazon in various geographies and on Kindle.

4) करावलम्बनम् (KARAVLAMBANAM) - Authors - Sridhar Subbanna and V Srinidhi. This Sanskrit book deals with concepts and applications, especially grammar, to learn functional samskrta. The author provided review and technical support for its publication. This book is available only as a hard copy; the author may be contacted directly.

5) SECOND IIMPRESSIONS—Authors—Various. This book deals with campus life at the Indian Institute of Management, Bangalore, from 1996 to 1998. This collection of memoirs was co-authored with other batchmates and received editorial support from a core group of batchmates. It is only for circulation among the batchmates and their acquaintances.